NAOMI EISENSTADT
CAREY OPPENHEIM

PARENTS, POVERTY AND THE STATE

20 Years of Evolving Family Policy

POLICY PRESS SHORTS POLICY & PRACTICE

First published in Great Britain in 2019 by

Policy Press
University of Bristol
1-9 Old Park Hill
Bristol
BS2 8BB
UK
t: +44 (0)117 954 5940
pp-info@bristol.ac.uk
www.policypress.co.uk

North America office:
Policy Press
c/o The University of Chicago Press
1427 East 60th Street
Chicago, IL 60637, USA
t: +1 773 702 7700
f: +1 773 702 9756
sales@press.uchicago.edu
www.press.uchicago.edu

© Policy Press 2019

British Library Cataloguing in Publication Data
A catalogue record for this book is available from the British Library.

Library of Congress Cataloging-in-Publication Data
A catalog record for this book has been requested.

ISBN 978-1-4473-4827-6 (paperback)
ISBN 978-1-4473-4829-0 (ePub)
ISBN 978-1-4473-4828-3 (ePDF)

The right of Naomi Eisenstadt and Carey Oppenheim to be identified as authors of this work has been asserted by them in accordance with the Copyright, Designs and Patents Act 1988.

Cover design by Policy Press
Front cover: image kindly supplied by Getty images
Printed and bound in Great Britain by CMP, Poole
Policy Press uses environmentally responsible print partners

Contents

List of tables, figures and boxes

List of abbreviations

ACE	Adverse Childhood Experience
CASE	Centre for the Analysis of Social Exclusion
CSJ	Centre for Social Justice
CYPU	Children and Young People's Unit
DCSF	Department for Children, Schools and Families
DfE	Department for Education
DfEE	Department for Education and Employment
DfES	Department for Education and Skills
DUP	Democratic Unionist Party
DWP	Department for Work and Pensions
ECCE	Evaluation of Children's Centres in England
ECM	Every Child Matters
EEF	Educational Endowment Foundation
EIF	Early Intervention Foundation
EMA	Education Maintenance Allowance
FIP	Family Intervention Project
FNP	Family Nurse Parntership
HBAI	Households Below Average Income
HLE	home learning environment
HMT	Her Majesty's Treasury
IFS	Institute for Fiscal Studies
IPPR	Institute for Public Policy Research
IY	Incredible Years
MCS	Millennium Cohort Study
NESS	National Evaluation of Sure Start

NHS	National Health Service
OECD	Organisation for Economic Co-operation and Development
Ofsted	Office for Standards in Education, Children's Services and Skills
ONS	Office for National Statistics
QED	quasi-experimental design
RCT	randomised control trial
SES	socio-economic status
SETF	Social Exclusion Task Force
UC	Universal Credit

Notes on the authors

Naomi Eisenstadt is currently a visiting research fellow at the International Inequalities Institute at the London School of Economics. She has spent the last four years working for the Scottish government on poverty issues, first as the Independent Advisor on Poverty to the First Minister and more recently as deputy chair of the Poverty and Inequality Commission for Scotland. After a long career in the non-governmental organisation (NGO) sector, Naomi became the first Director of the Sure Start Unit in 1999. The Unit was responsible for delivering the British government's commitment to free nursery education places for all three and four year olds, the national childcare strategy, and Sure Start, a major programme aiming to reduce the gap in outcomes between children living in disadvantaged areas and the wider child population. After Sure Start, Naomi spent three years as the Director of the Social Exclusion Task Force working across government to identify and promote policies to address the needs of traditionally excluded groups. After retiring from the civil service, Naomi was an Honorary Research Fellow at the University of Oxford for nine years. She chaired the Camden Equalities Commission and the Milton Keynes Child Poverty Commission, and published a book and several articles relevant to child development and child poverty. She was awarded an honorary doctorate from the Open University in 2002 and became a Companion of the Bath in 2005.

Carey Oppenheim is currently a visiting research fellow at the International Inequalities Institute at the London School of Economics. She also works for the Nuffield Foundation, leading a cross-cutting project on early childhood. Her previous roles include being the first Chief Executive of the Early Intervention Foundation, a charity and What Works Evidence Centre. She was Co-director of the Institute for Public Policy Research between 2007 and 2010, and special advisor to the former Prime Minister, Tony Blair MP, in the Number 10 Policy Unit between 2000 and 2005. She worked closely with ministers, civil servants and stakeholders on child poverty and children's rights, work–life balance, and social security and employment policy. Carey has also been a senior lecturer in Social Policy at South Bank University, as well as Acting Deputy Director and Head of Research at the Child Poverty Action Group. She chaired the London Child Poverty Commission, which developed policies to tackle poverty in the capital city. Between 2010 and 2013, she trained to be a teacher and taught history and politics at an inner-city London school. Carey is a member of the Social Metrics Commission, an independent charity, whose aim is to develop new poverty metrics in the UK that have long-term political support. She lives in London with her husband and their two daughters. She is writing in a personal capacity.

Acknowledgements

Many colleagues and friends were very helpful to us in writing this book. We are particularly grateful to Professor John Hills and Dr Aaron Reeves for accepting us as Practitioner Fellows at the International Inequalities Institute (III) at the London School of Economics. We also wish to thank the Joseph Rowntree Foundation as funders of these fellowships. The fellowships allowed us time together to work at the III, use all of the LSE's remarkable resources and meet with other fellows working on issues of social justice. Liza Ryan welcomed us to the III and helped us navigate the complexities of the university's systems.

Many people helped us with comments on early drafts, conversations on what we are trying to communicate and advice on other areas to consider for the book. John Hills chaired a roundtable discussion attended by Chris Cuthbert, Lisa Harker, Leon Feinstein, Donna Molloy, Tom Rahilly, Kitty Stewart and Kathy Sylva. It was extremely useful to share a range of views with such an expert group. Others who provided invaluable feedback were Kirsten Asmussen, Jabeer Butt, Jo Casebourne, Mubin Haq, Gavin Kelly, Tom McBride, Teresa Smith, Philippa Stroud, Teresa Williams and Jane Waldfogel. While we are grateful to all who provided advice and comments, any errors or misjudgements in the book are entirely ours.

ONE
INTRODUCTION

The title of this book reflects three of the key debates of post-war Britain: the roles of mothers, fathers and the wider family in bringing up children; the nature of poverty; and the role of public policy in both family life and tackling poverty. The book aims to provide an overview of family policy and how it has changed during the last 20 years; to set out the evidence base on factors influencing children's and family outcomes; and to assess how well policies address the reality of parenting and family life.

Through the lens of poverty, we analyse the attempts that successive governments have made to improve outcomes for children by reducing pressures on families and increasing the capabilities of parents and children. We argue that both are essential: reducing pressures by reducing child poverty; and improving capabilities by providing adequate support for parents and children. We have chosen to focus on children's outcomes that are most amenable to the influence of parents, in particular, children's cognitive and social and emotional skills, which mould their life chances as children, young people and adults. Therefore, we look mainly at policies aimed at parents but include some, like childcare, that can be seen as policies to improve child capabilities while also reducing pressures on parents. We concentrate on the lens of poverty because of its strong relationship with long-term outcomes for children, but we accept that strengths and risks occur across all social classes.

These areas of social policy have changed beyond recognition since 1945. We particularly concentrate on the last two decades, reviewing changing socio-economic/demographic trends, public attitudes, behaviours and government policy from the beginnings of New Labour in 1997 through to the Brexit-plagued Conservative government of 2018. Why these three issues?

Parents

Eminent child psychiatrist Sir Michael Rutter was once asked what advice he would give to a child growing up today; 'Choose your parents wisely', he said.[1] It is difficult to overstate the importance of the role of mothers and fathers on child outcomes. There is no doubt that schools can and do make a difference, and children's own individuality has an impact on outcomes; a combination of genetic predispositions, early environment and wider support systems beyond the immediate family all matter to child outcomes. However, what mothers and fathers do matters the most. The disposition to be a 'good parent' is influenced by one's own childhood experiences, as well as one's economic and social circumstances as an adult. Poverty, as will be discussed throughout this book, plays a very significant role not only in the practical ability to provide what children need for a healthy start, but also in terms of the energy expended on just getting by. Skills and techniques for managing tantrums in two year olds may be very useful but a parent's ability to absorb the appropriate skills may be limited by their pre-eminent concern about paying the rent, buying new school uniforms or paying for the class trip. Adequate income not only provides a basic living standard, but also fosters choice and agency. As the path-breaking research by Michael Marmot (Marmot et al, 1991) showed, there are long-term health consequences for those whose lives are typified by low levels of control and choice in work and in their day-to-day lives. Agency enables individuals and families to plan for the future, to consider options beyond the here and now. It empowers people to make decisions that may mean sacrifice in the short term but security in the longer term. Marmot's research found that such agency is correlated with life expectancy, as well as the likelihood of more years in good health. Parents with less money may make sensible decisions on a day-to-day basis that may result in poorer outcomes in the longer term. It is easier to give children what you know they will eat even if you know that it is less healthy rather than giving them healthier options that may immediately result in hungry, grumpy children, as well as unaffordable food waste.

The increasing emphasis on parents and what parents do with and for their children has masked what is a highly gendered debate about mothers, women in the workforce and the changing role of fathers. Unless explicitly aimed at fathers, it is mothers who most often participate in the wide variety of programmes that have emerged over the last two decades designed to improve *parenting*. Successive governments have come to understand how crucial parenting is to good or bad outcomes, and have therefore developed strong narratives, as well as investment in family support. A major part of the rationale has been that by improving parental capabilities, particularly when children are very young, those children will not need more expensive ameliorative services later in their school years and beyond. The focus for such support has most often been mothers living in poverty. The expectation has been that with the right start, children growing up in poverty can achieve upward social mobility, do well at school, get well-paying jobs and raise healthier children. These arguments have been woven into family policy discussion over the last two decades.

Poverty

Poverty has been a major topic for public debate since the Elizabethan Poor Law. Interesting from our perspective was

President Lyndon Johnson's War on Poverty in the mid-1960s in the US. The Johnson approach has echoes in the Blair/Brown approach of New Labour and reflects the strong influence of social policy from 'across the pond' on New Labour's agenda. Johnson combined improved benefits and income transfers with improved public services. It was under the Johnson presidency that Head Start was created, a major programme aimed at preschool children in poverty to improve school readiness. Like New Labour, many of the Johnson reforms have been dismantled, but the commitment to Head Start has survived. Many of the Labour reforms have also been dismantled, particularly those focused on reducing income poverty and a significant weakening of Sure Start, Labour's flagship programme for families with young children with aims similar to Head Start. However, the basic infrastructure of early years care and education, as well as work–life balance policies, have survived and, indeed, been expanded. Both the US and UK pursued anti-poverty strategies aimed explicitly but not exclusively at families with young children. The rationale was, and continues to be, that poverty damages children and poor child outcomes create intergenerational disadvantage, which is a drain on the economy. Reducing poverty through income transfers and employment policies or providing services that aim to ameliorate the impact of poverty on children have been key features of government policy for the last 20 years. Indeed, some of the examples of interventions in this book, like High Scope Perry Preschool in the US, have gained enormous traction because they have demonstrated value for money. Investing in services for poor young children saves money in the longer term on compensatory services, and yields a return in terms of a better chance of those children growing up to be productive tax-paying adults. In 1997, there were very high levels of both child poverty and pensioner poverty. Both these groups were seen to be the deserving poor. The attention to child poverty, as described earlier, was seen not only as an investment for the future, but also as a moral imperative. Chancellor Gordon Brown described child poverty as 'a scar on the soul of Britain'.[2] The attention on poor pensioners was a fairness argument; they had worked and contributed through tax and national insurance throughout their working lives and so deserved security in old age. Political pragmatism also played a role; people of pensionable age are most likely to vote.

Until quite recently, the debates on poverty have taken place in the absence of a discussion on inequality. Inequality describes the gap between those in the highest and lowest socio-economic or income groups and how that affects a range of social outcomes across social classes. Comparing children from low-income families to the rest implies that there is a clear cut-off point above which most children are fine. The data on income, social class and child outcomes tell a more nuanced story. The *social class gradient* (Wilkinson and Marmot, 2003) shows us that on almost all outcomes – health, education, social well-being and others – the bottom quintile (fifth of the population) does worst, the second quintile slightly better than the bottom but slightly worse than the third quintile, and so on. It illustrates that need is not just found in the poorest 20 per cent, but goes across the population. The odds of poor outcomes are highest for the poorest, and lowest for the richest. These odds are also influenced by other family factors like unemployment, poor housing, adult mental health problems or a family member with disabilities. This is important for two reasons. Assuming that it is only poor children at risk means that many families may not get the support they need. It also leads to stigma and the stereotyping of families in poverty. Most poor families do not have a set of complex and deep-seated problems. Some wealthy families raise children who have severe and life-changing problems. Poverty is an amplifier of the risk of poor outcomes; hence, reducing poverty should, in itself, reduce the likelihood of poor outcomes. The distribution of problems is weighted across social class quintiles, but risk as well as resilience is found in all groups.

Family policy and the state

What is meant by *family policy* and how have successive administrations since 1997 adapted and refined their responsibilities for the family? Family policy is a wide area, covering both social and economic policy. It includes employment legislation on maternity, paternity and parental leave, as well as tax incentives for marriage, child benefit rates and local housing policies that prioritise families with children over working-age single adults. Nested within family policy are particular policies concerned with parents and their responsibilities. For example, parents must ensure that children go to school, and they should ensure that children get the right inoculations at the right time. Parents are legally obliged to supply a base level of care, below which they can be found guilty of neglect. These responsibilities are different from interventionist policies designed to help mothers and fathers do the *job of parenting* better. They include universal and targeted services that encourage parents to engage with their children, for example, reading and singing to babies, taking trips to the library, and enquiring about homework. As will be described in Chapter Two, such advice can be fraught with danger for politicians who want to avoid the nanny state; it can be a field day for politicians who believe that the state can do everything. Advice on parenting can rub against powerful cultural norms and religious practices. Gender roles, physical punishment and attitudes towards homosexuality are all deeply rooted in cultural identities. While public attitudes on these issues have changed dramatically over the last 20 years, deep divisions between groups have emerged. Navigating between what research tells us is best for children and protecting the rights of parents to raise their children as they see fit can lead us into choppy waters.

Virtually all politicians enter the profession in order to change society for the better. Improving the lives of citizens, or, indeed, creating the conditions under which people can improve their own lives, is a key driver across all political parties. There is often little difference in these very broad goals between parties of the Right or Left but big differences in the underlying ideology that informs policies needed to achieve the goals. No one would argue that a strong economy is not good for most people; however, arguments will rage about achieving a strong economy through more or less market regulation. There is little argument that high-quality education plays a major role in improving individuals' lives, as well as the nation as a whole. However, there continue to be strong arguments about how to ensure that a good-enough education is available for all: grammar schools or comprehensive education; reducing the tax privileges of private education; or providing bursaries so that poorer children can be educated with the elites. Furthermore, public policy is not just about the central state. It includes other key actors: local government, city mayors, the voluntary sector, the private sector and citizens themselves. Local government is often left with the challenge of delivering policies imposed on it from the centre without adequate funding. This may lead to the reduction of discretionary services that local actors believe are more important for the local population. The voluntary sector plays a powerful role in both service delivery and advocacy for particular interest groups. The private sector is critically involved both as an employer and through the influencing role it has on employment rights, living wages and parental leave, and increasingly as the provider of some services, including some social services and some parenting programmes.

Political parties have had strong ideological differences about the nature of the state's role in relation to poverty and inequality. The last Labour government shifted its emphasis from equality of outcome to equality of opportunity. Labour was deeply committed to reducing poverty and improving social mobility while challenging the perception of a dependency culture. Labour wanted to provide *a hand up, not a hand out*; they believed that welfare rights go together with responsibilities. The Coalition and Conservative governments shifted away from the reduction of poverty as a goal of policy and chose to concentrate solely on social mobility. Like Labour, they argued that the socio-economic status (SES) of one's parents at birth should not be the determining factor of one's success as an adult. However, there was a sharp contrast between those deserving support and those not willing to help themselves. Chancellor George Osborne famously talked about helping the *strivers, not the shirkers*, a sharpening of the political rhetoric on welfare. However, no political party has been willing to articulate a vision of intergenerational social mobility where the outcomes of some children are lower than what would be expected given their social background. For relative mobility, space needs to be made at the top, so some may need to go down in status and income. Garrison Keillor expressed this irony in his wonderful radio broadcast about the imaginary town in Minnesota, Lake Wobegon, a place where 'all the women are strong, all the men are good-looking and all the children are above average' (Keillor, 1974).

Systemic issues of poverty, poor housing and low wages have come to be seen by some as irrelevant to child outcomes; it is only the behaviour and practices of parents that matter. Some politicians and commentators have come to believe that any parent can produce happy productive offspring if only they try hard enough. This implies that some parents just do not try. Much of the research described in this book dispels the myth that money and family resources do not matter to child outcomes. However, other personal and contextual factors matter as well.

Reducing pressures, increasing capabilities

The premise of this book is that public policy serves two primary roles in supporting families: *reducing pressures* and *increasing capabilities*.[3] Reducing pressures includes:

8

- fiscal and employment policies to increase incomes;
- benefit systems to even out differential income between families and to provide support across the life course as pressures increase or decrease;
- decisions on what types of families get what kind of financial transfers; and
- work–life balance policies to enable parents to spend time with their children.

Some policies do not involve direct income transfers, but reduce pressures by lowering the costs and risks of taking up employment. Examples of these policies include the provision of subsidised or free childcare and the right to return to a comparable-level job after maternity leave. Childcare, if of sufficient quality, can also be seen as a service to increase capabilities, albeit for children rather than parents. Other policies designed to improve capabilities include the provision of advice services and support for parents, structured programmes, health visiting and midwifery services that offer information, and skills development. Many services provided by central or local government, the voluntary sector, and the private sector can both reduce pressures and increase capabilities. Throughout this book, we use this framework to describe a range of policies and interventions concerned with families.

Finally

This territory is broad and complex and this short book cannot hope to cover it all. We do not cover Scotland, Wales and Northern Ireland, or regional differences, as this would require a book of its own. Neither do we go into detail on education policy, an area of active state intervention over the last two decades. We exclude it mainly because of space but also because it has largely been crafted with little reference to parents. As will be described in Chapter Four, the most radical restructuring of children and family support services, Every Child Matters, did not include schools policy. We have also had to limit discussion on more specific equalities issues such as disability, race and ethnicity, and gender. These clearly have strong relevance to discussions about poverty and parenting, and we hope that the analysis we offer and the examples we describe illustrate some of the particular issues facing some groups. Family justice policy is discussed only briefly, again because space does not allow an exploration of such a complex area.

Throughout this book, we argue that money is essential but not sufficient to improve outcomes for children from low-income families. The changes to the Child Poverty Act 2010 described in Chapter Four were a key driver in the motivation to write the book. We also argue that high-quality support services for parents and children can make a difference. If poverty is a key driver of poor outcomes, should we only concentrate on income transfers? If services that improve *parenting* can ameliorate the impact of poverty, do we perhaps only need to provide more and better services? Getting the balance right between the two approaches is fiendishly difficult.

Chapter Two of this book will describe the context of family policy over the last 20 years: changes in socio-economics, demographics, public attitudes and how we view parents and parenting. Chapter Three looks at the evidence about what makes for a good childhood and the role of socio-economic and family factors that predict better or worse chances in adult life. Chapter Four gives a detailed review of government policies on family and poverty, particularly how it changed after the 2008 crash and then through the Coalition and Conservative governments. Chapter Five offers an analysis of the effectiveness of some of the key policies: what worked and what did not, and why some strategies seemed to be more effective than others. Chapter Six provides a summary of what we have learned and an analysis of cross-cutting themes and building blocks for the future. What should be the role of government? Where can it most usefully intervene? Where is intervention likely to fail?

Notes

1 See: www.eif.org.uk/blog/choose-your-parents-wisely/
2 See: http://news.bbc.co.uk/1/hi/uk_politics/394115.stm
3 Thanks to Axel Heitmueller for his articulation of this framework to view family policy.

TWO

CHANGING IDEOLOGIES, DEMOGRAPHICS AND ATTITUDES

This chapter provides the context in which public policy on poverty, the family and parenting has evolved over the last 20 years. It examines changes in ideology in relation to the family, key socio-economic trends and shifts in public attitudes over the period, and why they are significant for family policy. The socio-economic trends we focus on include changes in economic growth, family type, the employment patterns of parents, housing tenure and costs, and the diversity of the population of Britain. These areas were chosen because they represent major changes, particularly in the lives of low-income families. They also provide the context for understanding the rationale for policy action. Finally, the chapter explores how this context has influenced parents' roles and the emergence of *parenting* as a concept in its own right.

Changing ideologies

Family policy has evolved over centuries, responding to as well as attempting to influence the behaviours of mothers and fathers. The state has concerned itself with matters such as marriage, divorce, the birth rate and parental responsibility. However, historically, the state has been reluctant to intervene directly in behaviours *within* the family, except where there was significant danger to children. The year 1997 marks the beginning of a significant change in the role of public policy in family life.

The Beveridge post-war welfare state was concerned with both the economics of the family and the birth rate. It created a social insurance system, underpinned by a National Health Service (NHS), tax-funded allowances for children and a commitment to full employment. It was also designed to prevent destitution and ensure a safety net for families. Beveridge's vision enshrined a traditional view of women's role, assuming that after the very active part women played during the Second World War, married women would and should return to the home as housewives. Alongside this was a concern about a falling birth rate; in Beveridge's words, mothers had 'vital work to do in ensuring the adequate continuance of the British race' (Cmd 6404, 1942). He proposed incentives for marriage and childbirth, and while his proposed marriage grant was not implemented, a maternity grant and benefit were introduced alongside widows' benefits and family allowance, becoming foundations for our current welfare state (Timmins, 1996).

All the main political parties embraced a post-war model of the nuclear family with one male breadwinner supported by a wife looking after two children (Kamerman and Kahn, 1997). Along with the traditional construction of the nuclear family was an assumption that the state's role in family life beyond economic welfare was limited to protecting children at risk of severe abuse. Fear of the nanny state was common across the political spectrum. The libertarian Right took an individual liberty approach aiming to limit the control of the overarching state on private lives. On the Left, there was concern that interference in families could disrupt the vital role of family members and communities supporting each other across generations. Other factions on both the Right and Left have always been more interventionist, wanting to tell mothers and fathers what to do: from advice on breast feeding to concerns with the prevention of youth crime. Advice varies from how to achieve the best for children to how to avoid the worst. Much of this book describes how that advice increasingly turned into public policy delivered through funding streams for income transfers, services, specific interventions and sometimes legislation. Such policy change was responsive to wider social change in the structure of families, though often with a significant time lag. The policy changes that we consider for this book were aimed at either reducing pressures on families or increasing parent capabilities. Some managed to do both and some failed at both.

Changing socio-economic trends

Boom and bust

An important backdrop to the ebbs and flows of family policy is the state of the economy. During the last 20 years, we have witnessed a long period of growth that began under John Major's administration in the mid-1990s and was built upon by Labour until the global financial crash of 2008, the largest financial crash since the 1930s. A recession followed but was mitigated by public investment between 2008 and 2010. Then followed austerity, with a substantial reduction in public spending under the Coalition government in 2010 and continued under subsequent Conservative administrations. Figure 2.1 shows the growth and decline of average gross domestic product (GDP) per head over the period. In 2009, we see a sharp fall of 4.9 per cent in GDP per head over the previous year. Over the same period, we see a rise in gross median real wages until the run-up to the financial crash but then a substantial fall and stagnation until very recently, when median wages have started to pick up (Social Mobility Commission, 2017). The economy both drives and responds to policy; decisions about how to respond to the financial crash and about public spending reductions and their focus are political choices, which have had important implications for families and children over this period. We explore the impact

Figure 2.1: Gross Domestic Product (average) per head year-on-year growth rate % CVM SA (1992–2018)

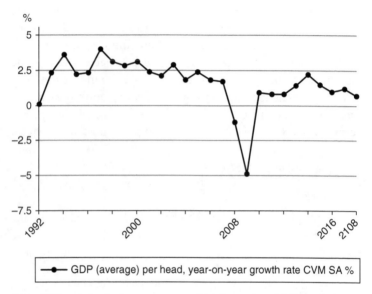

Note: CVM = chained volume measure, which is a series of GDP statistics adjusted for the effect of inflation to give a measure of 'real GDP';
SA = seasonally adjusted.
Source: ONS (2019), available at: https://www.ons.gov.uk/economy/grossdomesticproductgdp/timeseries/n3y6/pn2

of these decisions on family policy and families themselves in Chapters Four and Five.

Changing families

Family patterns have changed dramatically since the Second World War. Increases in divorce and remarriage rates, lone parenthood, and cohabitation, as well as the introduction of civil partnerships and gay marriage, have created a much greater diversity of family forms. Changes in public attitudes, as well as in policy, have made it easier for gay and lesbian couples to foster, adopt or have genetically connected children. This diversity reflects greater freedom and choice for parents to choose their own way of raising a family and expressing their sexuality. As we see in Chapter Four, family policies are changing to respond to this new diversity, but challenges remain, especially for families at risk of poverty.

Looking at trends over the last 20 years, we see a decline in the proportion of married-couple families with children and a doubling of the proportion of cohabiting couples.[1] Meanwhile, the proportion of lone-parent families has stabilised at 22 per cent of all families over this period.

These trends have implications both for families' risk of poverty and for the context in which parents carry out their roles. Some family types are more at risk of poverty, notably, lone-parent families. Separation and divorce can be a driver of poverty; a family managing in one household is likely to suffer a drop in income when separation requires two households (De Vaus et al, 2015). Lone parents – nine out of ten of whom are women – are twice as likely to be in poverty as couples with children. They are less likely to be in paid work and only 38 per cent of lone parents receive maintenance from a previous partner (Maplethorpe et al, 2010). Lone parents are also more likely to have someone with a disability living with them at home – 22 per cent compared with 18 per cent of couple families (ONS, 2013). Lone parenthood brings the challenges of not only a greater risk of poverty, but also managing children alone or in shared care arrangements with a non-resident parent. In summary, lone parents face a triple bind of low income, poorer job prospects and policies that fail to take account of their additional life pressures (Nieuwenhuis and Maldonado, 2018).

Cohabiting couples with children are also at greater risk of poverty; they are generally younger and have lower average incomes than their married peers. Both of these factors are associated with couple instability and hence contribute to the rise in numbers of never-married lone mothers.[2] Teenage parents, who make up a very small proportion of all parents, are much more likely to be in poverty than other groups. In 1997, the UK had high rates of teen mothers compared with most European countries. However, figures are now in sharp decline. This is the result of an ambitious long-term strategy kicked off in 1999 that included targeted interventions, a champion leading the strategy in every local area and a well-funded youth service. Such efforts coincided with a worldwide decline in teenage pregnancies as a result of increased education, improved access to reliable contraception and changes in social norms (Wellings et al, 2016).

Another feature of family life that has changed over the last two decades is that there are now one in four young adults aged 20–34 who are still living with their parents. This has grown from 2.7 million (21 per cent of this age group) in 1996 to 3.4 million (26 per cent) in 2017 (ONS, 2017). This change may be related to young people staying in education for longer, delaying formalising relationships and having children at older ages, as well as the increased costs of buying or renting a home. We explore some of the policy implications of this delayed transition to independence in Chapter Six.

Family life is dynamic and changes over the life course. Lone mothers often go on to form new relationships. The fluctuation in the separation and divorce of parents has led to a relatively modern phenomenon, that of *blended families*. These are families where the mother and father may bring with them children from previous relationships. They may then go on to have another child, creating a family of 'his, hers and our' children. This pattern will increasingly apply to same sex couples with children. For the individuals involved, including the children, the navigation of a complex set of relationships can be challenging. Evidence suggests that ongoing contact with birth parents is a protective factor for children in both divorced and separated families, as well as blended families, but arranging such contact can be both emotionally and practically difficult. The increasing numbers of gay and lesbian parents can bring new questions when it comes to separation and divorce. Decisions on residence and access will no longer default to the mother when there is no mother or there are two mothers. It is estimated that almost one in two children born today will experience their parents separating before they reach adulthood (Haux et al, 2015).

Families are not only about the relationship between parents or between parents and children, but also about sibling relationships and extended family members. Strong relationships between siblings and with extended families can be important sources of support, particularly at times of change and disruption. Family policy has had to catch up rapidly with the dynamic nature of modern family life. Changes in living circumstances and the numbers of children and adults in the household all have an impact on benefits and service entitlements. Chapter Three will discuss more fully what the impact can be of such changes on children, and Chapter Four will describe the changes in policy that have had to reflect modern family life.

Changing patterns of employment and poverty

Both the emergence of gender equality as a powerful social force and the increase in divorce, separation and mothers who have never partnered have had a significant impact on the numbers of women going into the labour market. So too have changes in the nature of the labour market, with the growth of low-paying and often part-time work in the service sector, creating more opportunities for those women who may prefer working part time but resulting in a long period of flat wages failing to keep up with inflation. The post-war assumption that one full-time wage could adequately support a family with children is long gone. Through the 1990s, there was a growing polarisation in the distribution of work between families with two earners and those with no earners (Gregg and Wadsworth, 1999). This led to increasing rates of child poverty, especially among lone mothers, and pushed policy under the Labour government towards more interventionist approaches encouraging both mothers and fathers into employment. Table 2.1 shows the increase in employment over the past 20 years, particularly for lone parents with children up to age 16, with a rise from 45 per cent in employment in 1996/97 to 68 per cent in 2016/17.

Despite record employment rates for both men and women in 2017, being employed no longer guarantees an escape from poverty. While it is true that the risk of poverty is highest for children living in workless households, the majority of children living in poverty now live in a household where at least one adult is in work. This is, in part, a reflection of the significant reduction in unemployment in recent years. Children in workless families are much more likely to be in persistent poverty than those in working families (Social Metrics Commission, 2018). Here, we define poverty as living below 60 per cent of contemporary median income after housing costs. This is the only available relative measure of poverty that covers the period from 1996/97 to 2017/18 (for a discussion of the Social Metrics Commission's approach to measuring poverty, see Chapter Five). Table 2.2 shows that in 1996/97, 56 per cent of children in poverty were living in a workless family and 44 per cent were living in a family where at least one adult was in work. By 2017/18, only 30 per cent of

Table 2.1: Rates of employment for mothers and fathers with children up to age 16 (1997–2016)

	1996/97	2016/17
Fathers in couple family	88%	92%
Mothers in couple family	68%	74%
Lone parents	45%	68%

Source: www.ons.gov.uk/employmentandlabourmarket/peopleinwork/ employmentandemployeetypes/datasets/workingandworklesshouseholdstable pemploymentratesofpeoplebyparentalstatus

Table 2.2: Percentage of poor children living in working and workless households after housing costs

	1996/97	2017/18
All poor children		
At least one adult in work	44%	70%
Workless families	56%	30%
Couple family		
Self-employed	11%	13%
Both in full-time work	1%	4%
One full time/one part time	4%	9%
One full time	15%	19%
One or both part time	6%	10%
Workless	21%	10%
Lone-parent family		
In full-time work	2%	6%
In part-time work	5%	9%
Workless	35%	20%

Source: Data tables, Table 4.3db: 'Composition of low-income groups of children by various family and household characteristics, UK', available at: www.gov.uk/government/statistics/households-below-average-income-199495-to-201718

poor children were living in a workless family while over two thirds (70 per cent) of poor children were living in a household with at least one adult in work. The failure of wages to keep pace with inflation and the increase in low-value part-time and/or insecure work has resulted in a marked increase in poverty for working families. Zero-hours contracts, frequently changing shift patterns and inconsistent income from week to week leaves families not only with inadequate income, but also with little basis on which to budget expenditure. Generous tax credits subsidising low wages did much to ensure that employment would reduce poverty for families with children in the early 2000s. Reductions in tax credits following 2010 greatly increased the risk of in-work poverty for families (Hick and Lanau, 2019). This has important implications for future policy, which needs to focus not only on worklessness, but also on how to improve opportunities and living standards for families in work. Overall, in 1997, one in three British children were living in poverty, one of the highest child poverty rates in the Organisation for Economic Co-operation and Development (OECD). By 2017, the child poverty rate was somewhat lower at 30 per cent.

Housing

A further major change shaping family lives, in particular, the lives of poor families, has been the dramatic changes in housing affordability and tenure. There have been sharp rises in the cost of housing relative to income. In the early 1960s, the average family spent just 6 per cent of their net income on housing; this had risen to 18 per cent by 2017. For the private rented sector, the increases are higher: from 9 per cent of net income in 1961 to 36 per cent currently (Cortlett and Judge, 2017).

The 'right to buy' introduced by Margaret Thatcher enabled council house tenants to buy their properties at reduced rates for the first time. This policy gave the chance of homeownership to thousands for whom it would not have been possible. However, it came at a cost. Local authorities who sold their stock of social housing were not permitted to use the receipts to build more public housing; hence, the supply of social housing declined dramatically during the 1980s and 1990s. Alongside the decline in the stock of social housing was the rapid increase in house prices. Over the last two decades, increases in house prices have outpaced wages by a large margin. Flat wages have made saving for a deposit to buy a home increasingly difficult. The 2008 crash was, in part, blamed on banks lending too freely. Hence, post-crash, it became more difficult to borrow for a mortgage. Table 2.3 illustrates the dramatic change in tenure

Table 2.3: Percentage of households with different types of tenure

Housing type	1997	2017
Owned outright	21.4%	27%
Mortgaged	34.1%	24.6%
Council-owned property	14.7%	7.2%
Housing association	3.7%	6.4%
Private rented sector	10.6%	18.4%

Source: www.resolutionfoundation.org/data/housing/

of households, with an almost doubling of the percentage of households now living in private rented accommodation. The private rented sector is notorious for short-notice increases in rent, poor property maintenance and frequent evictions. Between 1999/2000 and 2012/13, the proportion of private sector renters who were households with children increased from 22 per cent to 32 per cent (Chartered Institute of Housing and Resolution Foundation, 2014). Shelter (2013) estimates that one in five households now lives in privately rented accommodation; these families are more at risk of living in poorer conditions and experiencing greater insecurity, affecting children's access to stable schooling. Given the higher costs of housing in the private rented sector and the reductions in housing benefit, it is not surprising that there is a strong correlation between in-work poverty, as described earlier, and living in private rented accommodation (Hick and Lanau, 2017).

The picture is particularly bleak for homeless families, probably the poorest of all. While the number of households with dependent children accepted as homeless has declined dramatically from 66,290 in 1996 to 40,540 in 2016, the steady decline stopped in 2009 and numbers have been increasing in every year since 2010. Moreover, in 1995, 66 per cent of homeless families had dependent children. This had increased to 69 per cent of all homeless families by 2016.[3]

Finally, changes in housing benefit have hit the poorest families particularly hard. The introduction of the cap on overall benefits that families can claim has put extreme pressure on families in parts of the country where rents are very high. The cap, originally introduced at £26,000 per year and subsequently reduced to about £23,000 per year, set a limit on the overall benefits that any family could claim. It does not account for the numbers of children in the family, or, indeed, housing costs, although it is slightly more generous in London. Families with three or more children who need larger houses have disproportionately suffered.

A diverse population

Another issue that has had an impact on family policy has been the increase in the ethnic diversity of families. Immigration from the Caribbean, South Asia, Africa and, more recently, Eastern Europe has made the crafting of family policy, and particularly issues of appropriate and culturally sensitive intervention in family life, more complex.

In 1997, minority ethnic groups made up only 6 per cent of the population of England and Wales, and nearly half of the minority population lived in London; by 2011, the latest Census figures show that the figure rose to 13 per cent. The *Race disparity audit* (Cabinet Office, 2017) provides a detailed look at how different minority ethnic groups fare in the UK today. There are substantial differences in employment rates by ethnic group: one in ten adults from a black, Pakistani, Bangladeshi or mixed background are unemployed compared with one in 25 white British people. Pakistani and Bangladeshi groups are more likely to be in low-skilled and low-paying occupations than other groups. As a result, children from minority ethnic backgrounds are also more likely to be poor and in persistent poverty. Figures from 2016 show that 31 per cent of children from Asian and black ethnic groups were living in persistent poverty,[4] compared with 15 per cent of white British children. Until the 1980s, minority ethnic households were over-represented as owner-occupiers or as private renters. The trend in this century has been a decline in owner-occupiers from minority ethnic groups in comparison with white communities, as well as a significant growth in the private rented sector.[5] Minority ethnic families are also more likely to be living in homes of lower quality and in overcrowded conditions. This greater risk of poverty and discrimination for some minority ethnic groups has implications for children's future life chances.

Education has largely been a success story for most minority groups in Britain over the last two decades. Between 2006 and 2014, the percentage of key stage four pupils from a white British background decreased from 82 per cent to 75 per cent (Shaw et al, 2016). For areas with dense minority populations, including London, Birmingham and Leicester, the changes are even greater. In 1997 and, indeed, before, many schools in areas with large numbers of minority children were struggling with the number of children with little or no English. Often, English-speaking children had mothers who did not speak English. While professional advice urged teachers and early years workers to work with parents on their children's needs, language problems left teachers at a loss. However, more recently, in areas with high concentrations of minority ethnic groups, like London, the educational attainment of most minority group children has surpassed that of white British children. In terms of educational outcomes, England's poorest-performing children are, on average, white boys from low-income families. The socio-economic attainment gap is largest among white British pupils at all key stages. Disadvantaged young people from white British backgrounds are the least likely to access higher education, with only one in ten of the poorest attending university, compared to three in ten for black Caribbean children, five in ten for Bangladeshis and nearly seven in ten among lowest-income Chinese students (Shaw et al, 2016). There is some evidence that aspirational and ambitious parental influence has driven high performance in minority children, thus reinforcing other research showing that parents' behaviours and attitudes are a key component of good educational outcomes.[6] Despite clear educational success, the poorer employment rates and nature of jobs open to minority ethnic young people point to ongoing discrimination in the labour market.

The intersection of ethnicity and poverty has also had an impact on children's social care. Bywaters et al (2017) explored whether different groups of black and minority ethnic children were over- or under-represented in the care system. Contrary to previous studies, they found that black and Asian children were much *less* likely than white children to be on child protection plans or looked after when controlling for deprivation. In the authors' own words: 'Explanations for the disparities in intervention rates between White, Black and Asian children based on crude assumptions about family patterns or parenting need to be informed by the differential exposure to socio-economic disadvantage' (Bywaters et al, 2017). As minority ethnic children are more likely to come from economically disadvantaged families, they are over-represented in the social care system. Once poverty is taken into account, children from minority backgrounds are under-represented.

Some of the catastrophic failures by multiple state agencies have occurred, in part, because of attitudes to race and culture. Perceptions of cultural differences and unhelpful stereotypes have resulted in some professionals being reluctant to give advice to parents and carers for fear of offending cultural norms. The most extreme of these concerns was exemplified in child abuse cases, where it was found that social services and health services had missed indications of abuse because of presumed cultural differences that were often wrong. A seminal example was the death of Victoria Climbie (see Chapter Four). A combination of a failure of agencies to work together and assumptions about *cultural practices* was blamed for her tragic death. A failure to intervene out of respect for parents' or carers' culture left non-white children unprotected. The increase in minority ethnic staff in children's services has gone some way to reduce these difficulties.

However, a recent child abuse scandal with a race dimension has seen white children as the victims and mainly adult South Asian males as the perpetrators. A major contributory factor in the failure to protect these children was stereotypes about the abused children themselves rather than about the abusive men. Most of the victims were young girls who had either been in care or lived in chaotic households with limited parental supervision. They were seen as badly behaved young people making *lifestyle choices* rather than highly vulnerable, easily manipulated young girls. It has also been argued that there was a reluctance to intervene precisely because the majority of perpetrators were of South Asian origin. This could be a post hoc explanation given the over-representation of minority ethnic men in the rest of the criminal justice system. Undeniably, racial and social stereotypes and assumptions have resulted in the damaged lives of both minority and majority population children in the UK. It is important to note that these very high-profile cases represent only a very small minority of child abuse cases overall. Most cases of the physical abuse, neglect and/or sexual abuse of children happens within family groups and close friendship circles.

Living in diverse communities brings advantages for all children. Public attitude surveys have found that people living in diverse areas are much more likely to be comfortable with people of other backgrounds than those living in areas that are homogeneous (Schmid et al, 2014). Children growing up in Cumbria or Cornwall may be limited in their opportunities because they have not had the benefits of growing up in mixed communities. It is possible that their lack of experience of diversity may make them less eager to find work in Birmingham, London or Leicester, thereby limiting their horizons.

Changing attitudes

Alongside the changing socio-economic landscape, we have also witnessed important shifts in public attitudes that have shaped family policy. The British Social Attitudes surveys capture many of these changes.[7] For example, attitudes to sex, marriage and parents have shifted substantially. In 1989, 70 per cent thought that people who want children ought to get married; this had fallen to 42 per cent by 2012 (Park and Rhead, 2013). In 1998, 50 per cent thought that homosexuality was always/mostly wrong; in 2012, this figure had dropped to 28 per cent. Views of traditional gender roles have also changed.[8] In 1984, 49 per cent of the population held the view that it was a man's job to earn the money and a woman's job to look after home and family; by 2012, this figure had reduced to 13 per cent. There has also been a shift away from a preference for mothers to stay at home. In 1989, 64 per cent said that mothers of pre-school children should stay at home; this had fallen to a third (33 per cent) by 2012. In 2017, 38 per cent said that mothers with pre-school children should work part time and 7 per cent said that they should work full time. Interestingly, much of this change in attitudes occurred up until 2012 and has stabilised since then.

There have also been changes in public perceptions about poverty and those reliant on benefits over this period. There has been a long-running decline in the number of people who support the redistribution of income from the better-off to those who are less well-off, but since the financial crisis and austerity, support for redistribution is on the rise again (Hills, 2017). More than three quarters of people consistently say that income gaps are too large and most think that the government should do something about it (Hills, 2017). However, support for spending more on welfare benefits is much lower than it was 20 years ago, though there are signs of change; the latest British Attitudes Survey shows that one fifth of people support an increase in benefits for the unemployed, the highest since

2002 (Phillips et al, 2018). It also shows that in 2001, 39 per cent of people agreed that the generosity of welfare benefits creates dependence. In 2010, this rose to 55 per cent and has now dropped to 43 per cent, demonstrating a softening of attitudes towards welfare, but still not as generous as in 2001.

These shifts in attitudes come about as a result of a combination of factors (Park and Rhead, 2013). External events, such as the recession, shape people's views about unemployment. The political context and the prominent debates of the time also influence how people understand and interpret issues, as do changes in behaviour. For example, the rise in cohabitation is likely to shape views of marriage and relationships. Changes in attitudes may also come about because of the prevalence of certain groups in the population. We consider how these different factors have influenced family policy in Chapter Four.

The emergence of parenting

The interplay of changing ideologies, socio-economic patterns and public attitudes has shaped the roles of mothers and fathers, and catalysed a new debate on families: the importance of how mothers and fathers relate to their children and what they do with them. Ironically, at the same time as women have been increasing their hours of work outside the home, research evidence has been growing about the importance of the parent–child relationship and *parenting* to child outcomes (see Chapter Three). However, the public discourse on parents has moved from a descriptive relationship to an active verb; men and women are now expected to *parent* their children. The pursuit of gender equality in employment, the requirement for two incomes to financially support a family and increasing interest, if not pressure, to raise happy, healthy, productive children has created a perfect storm in terms of pressures on women to pursue well-paid careers as well as produce perfect offspring. Bookstore shelves are groaning with parent advice manuals, and the emergence of Netmums, Mumsnet and other social media forums for sharing advice and support for parents, usually mothers, is further evidence of the increasing concern that some of us may get it wrong, with drastic consequences for the next generation. Increasing capabilities has been a major feature of public discourse on parent*ing*, some of which has undoubtedly increased pressures on mothers and fathers to get it right. What constitutes good parenting is a subject of constant debate, from exhortations to allow children maximum freedom to grow and develop at their own pace, to the kind of drive for success typified by the stereotype of *tiger mothers* pushing children to ever-higher accomplishments. Chapter Three will give a fuller picture of what research indicates are the key components of good parenting.

Alison Gopnik (2016) has recently offered a challenge to the way in which parenting is viewed in her book *The gardener and the carpenter*: ' "To parent" is a goal directed verb; it describes a job, a kind of work. The goal is somehow to turn your child into a better or happier more successful adult, better than they would be otherwise.' Gopnik argues that *parent* should describe a fundamental relationship, like husband or wife, not an activity that should be learned and coached. She criticises an approach to parenthood which implies that the parent has the wherewithal to create the perfect human being. She considers that the danger in this approach is over-programmed children living highly scheduled and organised lives, lacking the freedom of emerging self-determination. Often, such well-intentioned but onerous efforts at *parenting* fail to produce the hoped-for results, leaving mothers and fathers feeling guilty and children and young people unhappy. Her gardening metaphor does not imply that parenting does not involve dedication and hard work; rather, it suggests that there will be many surprises and not everything growing exactly as intended. Gopnik is planting a traditional natural-looking English garden with space for wild flowers, not a formal, geometrically laid out French parterre. Any gardener will know that achieving the appearance of a natural and informal garden requires as much hard work, patience and dedication as the tidiest of lawns and sharply trimmed edges.

While these pressures affect all women, the impact on mothers in poverty has been particularly challenging. Child outcomes in health, education and life chances generally conform to the *social class gradient*. As described in Chapter One, poorer children do less well than their better-off peers, and middle-income children do less well than their richer peers. Successive governments have responded to the gap in outcomes between poor children and their better-off peers in different ways. Policies have been designed to reduce the numbers of children in poverty and to ameliorate the impact of poverty on poor children, improving their future life chances. Department for Work and Pensions (DWP) policies aim to encourage female labour market participation, reducing child poverty by increasing parental employment. When associated with generous working tax credits, this also succeeds in reducing pressures. However, since 2010, reductions in income transfers for lone mothers and couple families with children have increased rates of in-work poverty, as described earlier in this chapter. The Department for Education focuses on ameliorating the impact of poverty on children by improving schools and by building the capabilities of parents to provide the kind of home learning environment associated with improved child outcomes. These policies have resulted in increasing pressures on mothers in poverty to enter the labour market, to work more hours and to spend more time with their children. All these changes have probably not taken place without some cost to life satisfaction for mothers, fathers and children. Chapter Four explores policies that have reduced pressures through income transfers and improved leave arrangements, as well as those designed to improve capabilities through parenting interventions.

Finally, increasing public awareness about the importance of parenting behaviours for long-term child outcomes may have led to measurable changes in the time that both mothers and fathers spend with their children, despite increases in workforce participation. Using education as a proxy measure for class, time spent with children conforms to the social class gradient. Between 1995 and 2012, the number of minutes per day that university-educated mothers spent with their children more than doubled, from just over an hour per day to around 2.5 hours per day. Non-university-educated mothers in Britain also greatly increased the time with their children, but the amount of time was somewhat less than higher-educated mothers, from around an hour to just over two hours per day. Fathers also increased their time with children over the same period, albeit starting from a lower base. The gap between the fathers with degrees and those without degrees was wider than for the mothers in the two groups, and also widened over the time period. In 1995, British fathers with degrees spent around 50 minutes per day with their children. Fathers without higher education spent around 45 minutes per day. By 2012, better-educated fathers were spending just under two hours per day, while men without degrees were spending around 1.5 hours per day. All four groups experienced huge increases, but for both mothers and fathers, the education gradient increased (Dotti Sani and Treas, 2016). As described in Chapter Three, poverty itself can not only constrain time with children, but also have an impact on the kinds of activities more or less likely to encourage social and cognitive development (Cobb-Clark et al, 2016). Children benefit educationally from time spent with parents not only in the early years, but also right through school. The Effective Provision of Preschool, Primary and Secondary Education study showed that *academic activities in/outside the home are strong predictors of GCSE performance* (Sammons et al, 2014). Some of these activities involve significant expenditure: concerts, museum visits and holidays abroad. These results provide evidence that the emphasis on parenting without a parallel effort to reduce socio-economic inequalities may have caused a widening of the gap in outcomes between children from low-income families and their better-off peers (Del Bono et al, 2016).

Conclusion

The state is observer, recipient and shaper of social change. Changes in ideology, socio-economic/demographic factors, public attitudes and behaviour precipitated intense activity for government in relation to family policy. Public policy on the family has moved from a position of relatively benign neglect in the early 1990s to an increasingly interventionist approach. Chapter Four provides a detailed picture of how successive governments have responded to these changes in the landscape over the past two decades.

Notes

[1] See: www.nonmarital.org/Documents/Workshop_IV/Cohab_trends_UK.pdf

[2] See: www.nonmarital.org/DocumentsWorkshop_IV/Cohab_trends_UK.pdf

[3] See: www.ukhousingreview.org.uk/ukhr17/tables-figures/pdf/17–093.pdf [Table 93 Homelessness: categories of need in England]

[4] The Department for Work and Pensions (DWP) defines persistent poverty as when a person's income (before housing costs) has been below 60 per cent of the national median income in three out of the last four years.

[5] See: www.ethnicity-facts-figures.service.gov.uk/housing/owning-and-renting/renting-from-a-private-landlord/latest

[6] See: http://theconversation.com/against-the-odds-how-ethnic-minority-students-are-excelling-at-school-53324

[7] We draw on the British Social Attitudes surveys of NatCen Social Research; we have had to use varying time spans depending on the available data. For further reference, see: http://natcen.ac.uk/our-research/research/british-social-attitudes/

[8] See: www.bsa.natcen.ac.uk/media/38457/bsa30_gender_roles_final.pdf

THREE

WHAT DO CHILDREN NEED?

Over the last two decades, it is striking how evidence from a range of disciplines – psychology, economics, social policy, sociology and the biological sciences – has influenced both the debate and policies adopted to improve children's outcomes. Throughout this book, we look at two different types of evidence from research. In this chapter, we analyse evidence that is needed to understand how children develop and what shapes their outcomes, both positive and negative. The second type of evidence is the effort to find solutions to improving children's development or addressing their difficulties. In Chapter Five, we explore the evidence for the efficacy of responses to solve problems both at the policy level and at the practice level of particular interventions.

This chapter begins with some ground clearing to clarify key concepts and a brief overview of the phases of childhood development and recent breakthroughs in neuroscience that increase our understanding of development. Throughout the chapter, we focus on how poverty and family resources (material, social and educational) impact on child outcomes. We also look at the ways in which these socio-economic factors are mediated by family circumstances, parent–child relationships, the relationship *between* parents, maternal mental health and parenting practices.

We are particularly interested in the lens of poverty and policy. What disadvantages do children in poverty face? What impact do various factors have on outcomes for children in poverty? Can anything be done to improve the chances of better outcomes?

Key concepts and outcomes

There are a range of indicators of childhood development and outcomes that are related to lifelong well-being. They include early learning and school achievement, access to further and higher education, employment and healthy physical development, and mental health and well-being. They are also about staying safe – the prevention of child maltreatment, risky sexual behaviours, crime, anti-social behaviour and substance misuse. In this book, we are primarily concerned with the outcomes that are most amenable to the influence of parents, in particular, cognitive, social and emotional development. We chose these because children's cognitive and non-cognitive skills have a marked influence on a number of other outcomes in childhood and adulthood, from educational achievement to employment, income and physical and mental health (Marmot, 2010). We know, for example, that poor language and communication skills at the age of five are associated not only with weaker literacy and attainment, but also with a greater likelihood of mental health problems and unemployment in adulthood.

We draw upon different kinds of research evidence to understand what shapes these particular outcomes. The many research studies cited in this book use a range of different methods, including: randomised control trials (RCTs)[1] or quasi-experimental designs (QEDs),[2] which can be used to estimate the causal impact of an intervention; the analysis of longitudinal data that track the same group of individuals or households at different points in time; administrative data drawn from government departments or agencies; and qualitative research that provides insights into how or why a policy may or may not have been effective (HMT, 2011).

Our focus is on the relationship between family resources and child outcomes. Family resources include parental income (poverty and deprivation) and socio-economic status (SES), which includes parental education, occupation and social class. Sometimes, these are used interchangeably; however, as we will see later, in fact, each can have different impacts on particular aspects of children's development and their relative importance can change over time. It is also important to bear in mind that the influences on family life and children's outcomes – whether structural or psychosocial – are *dynamic*. Families and children move in and out of poverty, relationships may break down and re-form, and jobs are gained and lost. This moving picture of family life is best understood through longitudinal data and analysis. Building this data infrastructure is an important foundation for ensuring that policymaking is informed by how the patterns of children's and families' lives change over time.

The impact of family and other factors on child outcomes

The family has a primary and powerful influence on how a baby develops and fares throughout their childhood, into early adulthood and beyond. The way in which parents or caregivers nurture a baby, child and young person is affected by their own past, how they were brought up and the opportunities and adversities that they have faced, as well as the genetic inheritance and characteristics of their child. The love, nurture and care that mothers, fathers and other caregivers bestow (and, indeed, more rarely, their opposite: neglect and maltreatment) take place in a larger context. Parents and other family members, friends, the neighbourhood, the quality and accessibility of services, cultural and religious factors, and socio-economic circumstances all influence how a child develops. Bronfenbrenner's (1989) ecological model (see Figure 3.1) shows the different factors

Figure 3.1: Bronfenbrenner's ecological model

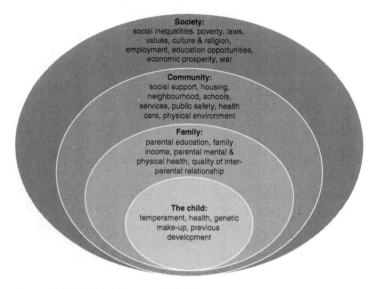

Source: Adapted from Asmussen (2011)

that impinge on a child's development. These factors change over the course of a child's life, marked by a series of significant transition points. It is a useful reminder that policies to support child well-being are more likely to be successful if they straddle societal, community, family and child factors, as well as take account of the developmental stage of the child.

Phases of childhood development

We know from a range of disciplines that *early* childhood matters; it is a particularly important phase of development. It is in this period that the building blocks for later development – physical, cognitive, language, social and emotional capabilities – are laid. 'Parents and other active caregivers are the "active ingredients" of environmental influence in the early childhood period'. How a child fares also depends on their parents' own health and well-being' (Shonkoff and Phillips, 2000).

We also know that inequalities in children's cognitive skills by socio-economic group are evident very early in a child's life (Feinstein, 2015a and 2015b; Jerrim and Vignoles, 2015). An early study by Leon Feinstein (2003) was highly influential in relation to the Labour government's *Every child matters* (DfES, 2003) policy and the Coalition government's social mobility strategy. This study included a graph which showed that, on average, children with low cognitive scores at 22 months of age in families with high SES improve their relative scores by the age of ten, while those who have high cognitive scores at 22 months but low SES worsen as they reach the age of ten (Feinstein, 2003). Commentary focused on the early years but, in fact, the shift in the scores occurs between the ages of five and ten. The Feinstein graph, as it came to be known, was widely cited and sometimes oversimplified in how it was interpreted and presented by policymakers and politicians.[3] However, the substantive point remains that SES shapes children's later progression from an early age. There is other strong evidence that gaps in children's cognitive skills can be observed early. In *Key competencies in early cognitive development: Things, people, numbers and words* (Asmussen et al, 2018), the authors show that there are income-related gaps across multiple areas of cognitive learning that begin before the age of three. Early Years Foundation Stage Profile results show a 9–18 percentage-point gap between children receiving free school meals and others across different early learning goals. While income plays a key role in early learning gaps, the authors identify a number of associated risks, including pre-term births and maternal mental health problems before and after birth. Early language development is vital for children's ability to communicate, manage their feelings and establish relationships, as well as for learning to read and write (Law et al, 2017). There are substantial differences in language acquisition by the age of two by income and gender.[4] Children in disadvantaged homes have significantly worse language acquisition than those in advantaged homes. However, gender has more of an impact than income, with boys doing worse than girls on early language development. Therefore, policies need to be sensitive to gender as well as to socio-economic and ethnic differences.

These gaps in cognitive skills, evident at an early age, do not decline through schooling; indeed, some research shows them as widening (Goldstein and French, 2015). Analysis for *An anatomy of economic inequality in the UK* (National Equality Panel, 2010) shows that the attainment gap between socio-economic groups widens between the ages of three and 14, and then narrows a little between the ages of 14 and 16 (Goodman et al, 2009). This pattern is similar for family income, fathers' occupation, mothers' education, housing tenure and area deprivation. However, the attainment gap between children from minority ethnic groups and white children has a completely different pattern. The gap in attainment between white and minority ethnic children at age three is larger than the gap between income groups, but by age 16, it has virtually disappeared. The gender gap narrows between the ages of three and five but then widens for older children.

Gaps in how children develop by socio-economic group are not confined to cognitive skills; they can be seen across a range of indicators, including health and behaviour (Marmot, 2010). Recent analysis of the Millennium Cohort Study (MCS) – a longitudinal study of 19,000 families in the UK collected since 2000/01 – shows that, on average, children who do not belong to low-income groups have better conduct and emotional health at the age of 11 than poorer children (Goodman et al, 2015). Boys are more likely to exhibit conduct problems but there were virtually no differences by gender in relation to emotional health. The socio-economic gradient in social and emotional skills was evident at the age of three and was likely to have started before that age, but it is hard to capture because of measurement difficulties. Importantly, this gap persists from the age of three until pre-adolescence.[5] These non-cognitive skills, still relatively neglected in policy and practice, matter for children's lifelong experiences. Drawing on the 1970 British Cohort Study, the authors show that children's social and emotional skills are associated with a range of improved outcomes much later on in adult life (age 42). Self-control and self-regulation are particularly important, being associated with adult mental well-being, good physical health and health behaviours, and positive socio-economic and labour market outcomes (Feinstein, 2015c).

Inequalities in cognitive and non-cognitive skills start early on in a child's life and appear to persist and, in some cases, widen through childhood and adolescence. Adolescence is a time of rapid development, with particular challenges. Recent data from the Centre for Longitudinal Studies[6] show the extent of mental health difficulties among young people. Girls and boys show similar rates of depressive symptoms at age 11, but as they approach adolescence, this rises substantially among girls – one in four girls report that they were depressed at the age of 14 compared to one in ten boys. Poorer mental health is more prevalent among teenage girls from poorer backgrounds, but not for boys. Being overweight, not getting along with peers and being bullied were all associated with poorer mental health.

While early childhood is a period of foundational development for children, each phase of childhood and adolescence comes with developmental milestones, risks and opportunities to improve life chances and narrow the gaps in outcomes between children growing up in poorer and more affluent homes. In the following section, we explore recent developments in neuroscience that confirm the need for policy solutions to focus not only on the early years, but also on adolescence and the transition into adulthood.

Brain development

One of the striking features in recent times has been the growth of neuroscientific research on different phases of child development and its influence on public policy narratives (for a discussion on the latter, see Chapter Six). While the research is still in its early stages, technological developments, such as magnetic resonance imaging, enable us to see the human brain at work, bringing important new knowledge as to how brains develop and function at different stages of life. There is not space here to do justice to this major field of study, but we draw out some of the important findings that have brought new insights and perspectives to understanding how babies, children and young people develop and mature.

There is no age limit on a brain's capacity to change; the ongoing capacity to change is known as experience-*dependent* plasticity (Blakemore, 2018). This is different from brain experience-*expectant* plasticity – or a sensitive period that begins at conception and levels off in adulthood. Brain development is particularly rapid and foundational from the point of conception and in the early years of a child's life; however, importantly, more recent research has shown that there are later critical periods in adolescence and young adulthood.

Early environments – physical, social and emotional – shape how a child's brain develops (Oates et al, 2012). This early period is one of particular sensitivity given the plasticity and responsiveness of the brain, establishing many of the specialised regions of the brain with functions such as language, emotions, memory, planning and attention (Oates et al, 2012). Before a child is born, exposure to drugs, alcohol, malnutrition and infection can detrimentally affect a baby's brain development. However, the development of the brain is not linear; it peaks at different times in the early years of a child's life, requiring 'age-appropriate' experiences to achieve optimal development (National Scientific Council on the Developing Child, 2007).

An example of how a child's early experience can impact brain development is shown in a recent trial on how children's exposure to conversation with an adult is associated with their language-related brain function (Romeo et al, 2018). We know that children's experience of early language at home has an impact on their later language and cognitive skills, and that there are substantial average differences by SES. This latest study illuminates the neural mechanisms in the brain that underpin this relationship. The study focused on 'conversational turns with adults', that is, two-way conversations that include not only linguistic information, but also non-verbal communication, such as responsiveness, attention and exchange with children aged four to six. It found that those who had experienced more conversational turns (and not simply the number of adult words) – independent of SES and intelligence quotient – showed greater left inferior frontal activation in the brain, 'which significantly explained the relation between a child's exposure to language and their verbal skills' (Romeo et al, 2018). The authors conclude that 'While causation cannot be implied, results suggest that early language exposure, a proximal aspect of children's environment, may alter the way in which their brains process language' (Romeo et al, 2018). The findings underline other research that shows the importance of encouraging this interactive aspect of language development in programmes to support parents and early years teachers.

Recent research shows that the brain continues to develop through childhood and adolescence, and into the 20s and 30s in some brain regions: 'Contrary to the received wisdom up to the late twentieth century, we now know that our brains are dynamic and constantly changing in to adulthood, and that the transformation they undergo in early life continues for far longer and has much bigger implications than previously thought' (Blakemore, 2018). During adolescence, the prefrontal cortex – the location in the brain for decision-making, self-regulation and self-evaluation – goes through profound changes. Blakemore illustrates the way in which young people's capacities and skills continue to develop at different stages. The cognitive skills of adolescents (aged 11–18) and adults (aged 19–33) were tested by getting them to practice a computer game over 20 days of online training. They found that all age groups improved their skills but that late adolescents (aged 16–18) and adults made most improvement. Blakemore argues that this makes this late developmental stage a particularly important opportunity for education and social development.

Neuroscience is throwing up powerful insights into what shapes a child's development. In some cases, it reinforces what we know from other disciplines but provides a new perspective on the mechanisms through which the environment can shape and influence a child's reactions, skills and capabilities. In other cases, it overthrows previous assumptions, for example, the view that the human brain does not develop much after mid- or late childhood. In some instances, it may help us to design interventions, such as the nature of interventions to support language development or when it might be best to teach certain cognitive skills. It is important to remember that while studies that use neuroimaging can tell us about associations between a change in the size of or activity in a part of the brain and, for example, a behaviour, state of mind or characteristic, they cannot tell us about causes or predict outcomes for individual children (Blakemore, 2018). We need to be careful not to overstate the science, which is still in its early stages.

The parent–child relationship

There is an extensive body of empirical evidence from a range of disciplines on how parents influence and impact on a child's development. However, what constitutes *good* parenting is inevitably a controversial subject. Asmussen (2011) argues that 'Most people have an implicit understanding of good parenting that goes beyond meeting children's physical needs. This understanding includes the provision of love, safety, educational guidance and economic security.' *Parenting* is also a normative concept that reflects context, time, culture and ideology. Services and programmes that aim to support the parent–child relationship feature strongly across all political administrations over this 20-year period. In this chapter, we focus on what the evidence tells us about what good parenting is and how it can help children to flourish. In Chapter Four, we look at how the concept of parenting has been used in different political and policy contexts.

While research shows the importance of child–parent *interaction*, the child's own characteristics and disposition are sometimes forgotten in policy discussion about parenting. Parenting is seen to be *done* to the child rather than a two-way relationship. We know that a child's disposition and characteristics influence mothers' and fathers' actions and responses. Despite the gender-neutral term 'parent', in practice, much of evidence and policy has focused on the mother, and only more recently have fathers been brought into the picture. The growth of lesbian, gay, bisexual and trans-gender families also challenges traditional gendered notions of parenting.

Both parenting practices and family resources (poverty, class and education) have a profound impact on child outcomes, but the interaction of family resources and parents' behaviours is complex. Here, we explore theories informed by developmental psychology. These theories have provided the foundation for the development of a range of parenting interventions and approaches, which are explored in Chapter Five. Looking first at parent–child interaction in the early years, we know that the relationship and interactions between parent(s) and child has a deep and lasting influence on a child's attachment, social and emotional development, and cognitive skills (Asmussen et al, 2016). How this happens remains a matter of controversy. O'Connor and Scott (2007) describe the three principal theories that link parent–child relationships and child outcomes: attachment theory; social learning; and parenting styles. Attachment theory focuses on the bond between a parent and child established from the very earliest stage; parental sensitivity and responsiveness to the child shapes the security of the attachment. Insecure-disorganised attachment is associated with an increased risk of mental disorders. Social learning theory describes how a child's behaviour is influenced by observation, imitation and the reaction that their own behaviours generate. In the early years, the family context is the primary source for this social learning.

Parenting style and practices are thought to be an important influence on child development (Asmussen, 2011). Four parenting typologies have been developed: (1) *authoritative* – high warmth, positive and with assertive control; (2) *permissive* – high warmth with low control; (3) *authoritarian* – low warmth, high conflict, coercive and punitive; and (4) *neglectful and disengaged* – low warmth and low control. Authoritative parenting styles have been associated with positive outcomes for children (Heath, 2009). Children growing up with authoritative parents were found to have higher levels of educational achievement, self-control, reasoning ability and empathy. They were also found to be more cooperative with adults and peers than children growing up in families with authoritarian, permissive or uninvolved parenting styles (Rutter et al, 1998). 'Helicopter parenting', as it is popularly called, is a more intense version of authoritative parenting. While some studies show that it can be associated with adolescent difficulties in relation to internalising and externalising disorders and lower self-motivation (Waylen and Stewart Brown, 2008), others show that an 'intensive parenting style' is correlated with high academic scores, controlling for parental education.[7] Other parenting styles are associated with worse outcomes, in particular, authoritarian parenting because of its coercive nature (O'Connor and Scott, 2007).

There has been an important critique of this analysis of parenting styles as failing to take account of differences of social class, gender and ethnicity (Phoenix and Husain, 2007). The authors explore how different meanings and outcomes may attach to the same parenting behaviour depending on ethnicity, social class and religion. Contextual factors such as local neighbourhoods also influence parenting practices. For example, for families living in high-crime areas, an authoritarian style of parenting may be essential for child safety. Understanding how parenting practices and their impact may differ between diverse population groups is vital if policy and interventions are to be effective for different groups.

Parenting styles can also vary between parents in a family and over time. Persistent conflict between parents can affect their ability to parent together – to co-parent – and this, in turn, impacts on children's outcomes. Pressures on families in balancing work and family life, especially in the context of both parents working, may result in parents feeling that they lack time, patience and availability to be with their children (Lewis, 2007). This points to the importance for policymakers in thinking about the relationship between family-friendly employment policies and parenting.

There has been new research on understanding the impact of fathers on child development. Fathers are spending more time with their children than previous generations of men, especially if they have a child aged under five (Faux and Platt, 2015). There has been some change in how fathers perceive themselves, from the breadwinner of the family to being an involved father, though still with a work identity (Dermott, 2008). Lewis and Lamb (2009) look at the importance of involved fathers, particularly for boys and adolescents. Not surprisingly, health, poverty and work pressures influence father–child interaction, as well as mother–child interaction, but the relationship between the father and the mother particularly influences a father's relationship with his child (see p.51).

There has been a growing focus on the relationship between parenting practices – specifically the home learning environment

(HLE) – and children's cognitive and social-emotional development. HLE includes a set of parenting practices that support the child's development: reading stories, singing, trips to the park or the shops, and regular meal times and bedtimes. The path-breaking Effective Provision of Pre-school Education (EPPE) study looks at the relative influence of family income, occupational status, parent education and HLE on children's early outcomes (Sylva et al, 2010). It shows how parents' income, social class and education are *each* independently associated with both cognitive and socio-emotional outcomes for children. However, the authors find that parental education is associated more strongly with child outcomes than either family income or SES (a finding that differs from work by Schoon et al [2013] discussed later). The EPPE study shows that both the mother's and the father's education is important but especially that of mother. Interestingly, they find that the quality of the HLE exerts a greater independent influence on educational achievement than income, SES or parental education. While families with lower incomes/SES tend to have a poorer HLE, this is only a moderate association. Poorer families sometimes have high HLE and vice versa. The authors conclude that improving the HLE may offer an important vehicle for improving all children's life chances. This bears out work undertaken by Kiernan and Mensah (2011), which showed that 58 per cent of children who lived in persistent poverty but had high parenting scores had a good level of achievement.

A later study by Washbrook, Gregg and Propper (2014) unpacks the pathways between family resources, parental behaviours and the child's lived environment to six different outcomes in middle childhood. It finds that income plays a direct role in relation to cognitive outcomes for children. Parental education is a powerful predictor of educational, behavioural *and* health outcomes for children. The authors suggest that financial resources may also play an indirect role via maternal mental health. Poor maternal mental health is associated with low income and poorer child outcomes. Immediate factors that account for significant portions of the gradients in child outcomes are harsher discipline, a more external locus of control[8] and lower rates of breastfeeding. The authors make clear that they are using observational data, so they cannot assume a causal relationship. However, their analysis throws light on potential targets for intervention. They suggest that it may be preferable to focus on an intervention that has modest effects across a range of outcomes rather than one with a larger effect on a single outcome. They also stress the importance of thinking not only about the relationship between the 'behaviour' and the outcome, but also about the extent to which the behaviour is concentrated among low-income families.

Family stability and relationships

There is a growing body of work on the relationship between family structure and instability on children's well-being. The importance of marriage and stable family relationships has been a strong feature of Conservative manifestos and policy – and was identified as one of the five key drivers of 'Breakdown Britain', an influential report produced by the Centre for Social Justice (see Chapter Four). Marriage is associated with better educational and socio-emotional outcomes for children. However, the Institute for Fiscal Studies (Crawford et al, 2013) found that the differences in cognitive and socio-emotional development between children born to married parents and those born to cohabiting parents were mainly or entirely due to the fact that different people choose to get married (that is, a selection effect) rather than that marriage itself has an effect on relationship stability or child development.

A recent study drawing on the MCS (Fitzsimons and Villadsen, 2018) has shown that children who have experienced their parents separating (whether they had been married or cohabiting) are 16 per cent more likely to experience emotional problems and 8 per cent more likely to experience conduct problems.[9] The timing of separation matters – early paternal departure when the child is aged three to five has no short-term effects on the child and only weak evidence of an effect in the medium term on girls. However, later departure in mid-childhood (aged seven to 11) is associated with an increase in internalising problems for both boys and girls, and externalising problems for boys alone. The research shows that when the father leaves the household, there are significant reductions in income, especially when children are older. It also shows that paternal departure is associated with detrimental effects on the mother's mental health.

Work by Schoon et al (2013), also using the MCS, explored the early influences on the well-being of children. They find that poverty, especially persistent poverty, over and above other factors, was associated with lower cognitive ability and behavioural development at the age of five (we explore this further on p.53). However, they also find that family structure and instability has an independent effect, particularly on emotional and behavioural adjustment.

Given the steady rise in divorce and separation, it is important to know how this affects contact between children and their non-resident parent, and the way in which separated mothers and fathers parent. Faux and Platt (2015) show that levels of contact are high, with eight in ten separated fathers in contact with their child. Fathers' involvement with their children prior to separation is associated with more frequent contact with their children after break-up. SES also influences whether there is any contact, with slightly less contact in lower socio-economic groups. Mothers who separate are more likely to experience maternal depression and higher rates of child behavioural problems, which, in turn, makes them feel less competent as parents (Faux and Platt, 2015). This suggests that policies to promote father involvement with their children are not only important for parents who stay together, but could also pay dividends for those who separate. Equally important is the need to address the mental health needs of both mothers and fathers, as well as children's behavioural difficulties, following separation.

The findings from the aforementioned studies might suggest that policy should encourage a return to more traditional family forms. However, this flies in the face of long-term trends of greater diversity of family forms and changing attitudes, as we identified in Chapter Two. Instead, a more fruitful policy direction would be to focus on interventions to support the quality of parental relationships, maternal mental health and children's social and emotional development where there is family conflict. Delaying childbearing, and improving stability in other aspects of children's lives, such as housing, schooling, childcare and employment are important.

More recently, the policy focus has shifted to the *quality* of the inter-parental relationship – rather than on family structure per se. Changing demographics and attitudes to non-traditional families, alongside new research on the importance of the quality of the parental relationship for child outcomes (Harold et al, 2016), all contributed to this important policy shift. Research on the quality of the inter-parental relationship (whether couples are together or separated) shows that it has a substantive influence on children's development and later life chances. Frequent, intense and poorly resolved conflict between parents can impact on a range of child outcomes, from child mental and physical health to educational attainment. The 'silence to violence' continuum (Harold et al, 2016) describes the fact that conflict does not necessarily have to be overtly violent – silent unresolved conflict can also be damaging. The Family Stress Model shows how the quality of the inter-parental relationship has both a direct impact on child outcomes and an indirect impact on child outcomes mediated through parenting (see Figure 3.2). A high degree of unresolved conflict between parents makes it more difficult to co-parent, and parenting interventions are less likely to be successful. Conflict between parents tends to be more

Figure 3.2: Family Stress Model

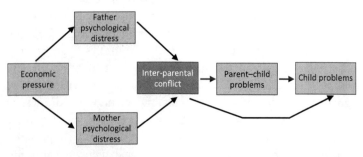

Source: Acquah et al (2017)

disruptive of the father–child relationship than the mother–child relationship, with fathers more likely to withdraw and mothers more likely to overinvest in the parent–child relationship (Harold et al, 2016). Mothers may be more able than fathers to separate out their roles as both partner and parent. Parents may also treat children of the opposite gender in a more negative manner in the context of family conflict and children, in turn, may identify more strongly with the parent of the same gender. While such conflict is damaging for both boys and girls, their responses differ. Family stress is associated with a greater risk of externalising behaviour for boys early on in their development, and with a greater risk of internalising symptoms for girls in adolescence (Harold et al, 2016).[10]

Not surprisingly, relationship distress is more common in families where both parents are not in work. Department for Work and Pensions (DWP, 2017a) figures show that relationship distress is around three times as prevalent if both parents are workless as compared to when both parents are working. Over a quarter (28 per cent) of all children living in workless couple-parent families live with parents reporting a distressed relationship. Further work has explored how poverty and economic stress affect the quality of the inter-parental relationship, and how this, in turn, impacts on child outcomes (Acquah et al, 2017). This is captured in the Family Stress Model (see Figure 3.2). Longitudinal evidence shows that economic pressure impacts on parents' mental health, which can, in turn, cause relationship problems and difficulties with parenting (Masarik and Conger, 2017). These difficulties can include reduced parental sensitivity and time spent interacting with their child, and can lead to harsher parenting practices, which are linked to future difficulties for children and adolescents.

Poverty and socio-economic status

There is an extensive body of work that shows the strong *gradient* of outcomes across SES and poor outcomes for children, including education, health and social and behavioural development. Looking at SES by quintiles (fifths), children in the bottom 20 per cent are likely to do less well than those in the 20–40 per cent quintile. Those in the top quintile are likely to score highest on indicators of children's school readiness. Vocabulary, conduct problems and hyperactivity each show a social gradient (Washbrook and Waldfogel, 2008). Younger parents may be on a low income because they are at the start of potentially lucrative careers. Moreover, this does not mean that all children from lower SES families will not do well or, indeed, that all children from better-off backgrounds are bound to succeed. Rather, it means that one's chances of doing well are, in part, shaped by the SES into which one is born. The gradient in childhood outcomes means that policy responses need to focus not only on the poorest children.

Disentangling income poverty from other factors that shape a range of child outcomes is difficult. Schoon et al (2013) find that family income is associated with children's cognitive and behavioural development over and above other interlinked risk factors: maternal age, parental education, social class, worklessness, housing tenure, family instability, area deprivation and the number of siblings. The timing and duration of hardship matters: the largest effects are for persistent poverty and when a child experiences poverty in the first year of life. Lower cognitive scores are associated with repeated episodes of poverty and exposure to other risks in the first year of life. The accumulation of a number of risks had the strongest impact on children's outcomes. Importantly, there are a number of protective factors that were associated with reducing the impact of low income on child outcomes, such as birth weight, gross motor development, warm parent–child interactions, regular bedtimes, reading to the child, going to the library and living in a good area for raising children with friends and family nearby. Breastfeeding was found to be particularly important for children's cognitive skills, and maternal mental health, regular bedtimes and non-harsh parenting discipline in relation to children's behavioural development. Formal and informal childcare were also important protective factors. The wider social context in which children are growing up plays an important role in their development. The authors propose a broad-based preventive approach that addresses living conditions as well as the cognitive, emotional, social and biological development of children.

The most recent research by Cooper and Stewart (2017) shows that household income has an independent impact on child outcomes, that is, that 'money in itself does matter'. Their research builds on an earlier review of international research, *Does money affect children's outcomes? A systematic review* (Cooper and Stewart, 2013). The review draws on a combined total of 61 studies that use RCTs, QEDs or analysis of longitudinal data. In combination, this enables the authors to establish a *causal* relationship between income and child outcomes. The evidence is particularly strong in relation to the impact of household income on children's cognitive development and school attainment, followed by the evidence on social, emotional and behavioural development and physical health (Cooper and Stewart, 2017). The authors explore the way in which income may shape child outcomes through *intermediate* factors. They find that increased income is associated with an improved HLE: more stimulation, parental responsiveness and supervision; more activities with the mother; and a reduction in parental stress. In one US study, families who had additional income (through additional child support payments) showed a reduced risk of child maltreatment (Cancian et al, 2013). The study also found strong evidence for increased household income improving maternal mental health, while moving into poverty was associated with a deterioration in mental health (Wickham et al, 2017). The impact of income on mothers' physical health and behaviours was more mixed, depending on the outcome in question. Not surprisingly, they found strong evidence for the importance of income on having enough food to eat. The authors found that 'effects from the most robust studies were found to be comparable in size to effect sizes for spending on school or early education interventions' (Cooper and Stewart, 2017). They also argue that policies to increase family incomes can benefit the whole family as well as the child, unlike investments in policies that are solely focused on the child.

Cooper and Stewart (2017) draw on two theories – what they call the Investment Model and the already mentioned Family Stress Model – to explain *how* income affects children's outcomes. The first of these is simply that parents need money to support a child's development: toys, books, trips, a space to play and study, and a nutritious diet. The second is that the lack of money generates stress for parents, affecting their mental health, which impacts negatively on how they parent. Economic hardship and pressure can lead to psychological distress, which, in turn, impacts on the relationship between parents and between parent and child. This relationship stress then influences child and adolescent outcomes.

Recent work by Cooper (2016) provides further insight into the relationship between economic hardship, parenting and child outcomes by looking at how parenting varies at different income levels. She finds that after controlling for the mother's education and work status, the majority of mothers were 'parenting in ways we would describe as good' (Cooper, 2016). In some areas, such as helping their child with writing and maths and taking their child to the park, low-income mothers did this more frequently than their better-off peers. However, in other areas of parenting, such as trips outside of the home, hours of television, nutrition[11] and bedtime routines, low-income mothers were doing worse. These differences persisted when using different measures of hardship. Cooper found that hardship defined as debt, deprivation and feeling poor was associated with mothers' mental health and life satisfaction. This then fed into worse parenting behaviours. For some aspects of parenting, such as discipline and play activities, mothers' mental health fully explained the relationship with hardship. In other outcomes – like routine mealtimes and bedtimes – mental health and the inter-parental relationship accounted for around half of the relationship. She concludes that the Family Stress Model explains some of the relationships between hardship and certain parenting behaviours and that the Investment Model explains others (Cooper, 2017). This suggests that policies that reduce poverty will also help to address maternal depression.

A third theory explores the relationship between socio-economic disadvantage, parenting style and human development through the impact that poverty has on parents' attention or cognitive effort (Cobb-Clark et al, 2016). It is argued that parents who are coping with poverty, financial difficulty and associated hardships are less likely to have the cognitive bandwidth to be able to attend to, engage with and monitor their children.

Income transfers are therefore important not only to address the direct effects of poverty on children's access to material and social resources, but also to mitigate the effects of poverty on parents' psychological well-being and cognitive bandwidth. Effective couple and parenting support also has an important role to play.

Families at high risk

Given the impact of poverty on children's outcomes, we should be particularly concerned about its extent and its depth. Although the government abolished the child poverty targets in 2016, it continues to publish data on the number of children living below various income thresholds (DWP, 2019). In 2017/ 18, there were 4.1 million children living in poverty – 30 per cent of all children (defined as living below 60 per cent of contemporary median income after housing costs). A much smaller number of children, 700,000 (5 per cent), are both in low income and have severe material deprivation (defined as living below 50 per cent of income before housing costs). The Joseph Rowntree Foundation (JRF, 2018) survey of destitution shows that in 2017, there were 1.5 million households with 365,000 children living in destitution. They define destitution as people who lack two or more of six essentials (housing, food, heating, lighting, clothing and footwear, and basic toiletries) over the past month because they cannot afford them. The drivers of this destitution are debt repayments, inadequate benefits and health problems. Destitution has declined by 25 per cent since 2015 when the first survey was undertaken, which the JRF attribute to a reduction in benefit sanctions, an increase in employment and a reduction in the numbers of migrants, who are particularly vulnerable to destitution.

There are a small proportion of children who experience multiple deprivation, including low income, material as well as non-material deprivation, and other family characteristics that are associated with poor outcomes. As will be discussed in Chapter Four, all administrations over the last two decades have been concerned with *high-risk, high-cost families*, and all looked for ways to identify and support these families. Here, we look at four approaches to capturing multiple risks faced by children and families that have been widely used in public policy or the delivery of services. It is important to bear in mind that each has been developed with a different purpose in mind. In the following, we describe the Social Exclusion Task Force (SETF) framework, the DWP's analysis of risks associated with workless households, the Adverse Childhood Experiences (ACEs) approach and the Children's Commissioner's vulnerability framework.

In 2004, the SETF in the Cabinet Office estimated that there were 140,000 families – 2 per cent of all families – who experienced multiple deprivation (SETF, 2007). Figure 3.3 shows how the risk of poor outcomes increases as the number of family disadvantages increases, for example, 1.4 per cent of children in families with no disadvantages were suspended or excluded from school in the previous year, compared with 11.1 per cent of children in families with five or more disadvantages. However, there are two important caveats in interpreting and using these data: first, there is a *gradient* in the proportion of children with poor life experiences that relates to the number of disadvantages they face; and, second, even in this very deprived group of children, the vast majority of children do not have these negative outcomes. As can be seen from Figure 3.3, while 10 per cent of children with five or more disadvantages were in trouble with the police in the preceding year, 90 per cent were not, and while 18 per cent of children ran away from home, 82 per cent did not. Moreover, in families with no risk factors, a small percentage of children still had poor outcomes (SETF, 2008).

The use of these data by policymakers has been problematic. It led to an assumption that there is a clear cut-off point where children with five or more disadvantages are defined as multiply deprived and those with fewer disadvantages are not. The figure of 140,000 families become entrenched in public policy as the target group for the Troubled Families programme; indeed, the number was then broken down into target numbers of families for each local authority to address. It was misleading to assume that the group was tightly defined and static, and therefore that if you were able to help this specific group, there would not be

Figure 3.3: Child outcomes by number of parent-based family disadvantages

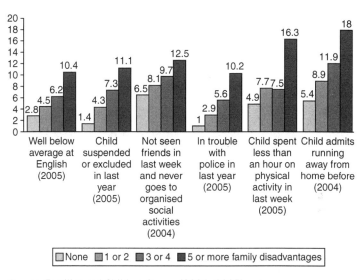

Source: Families and Children Survey (2004, 2005)

more families who would continue to need help (for a discussion of the Troubled Families programme, see Chapter Four). It also led to the inaccurate perception that the majority of children and young people in families facing multiple deprivation are in trouble with the police, running away from home or suspended from school. Such assumptions risk poor policies, the inaccurate targeting of services and stigma for the families targeted.

The DWP (2017a) publication *Improving lives: Helping workless families, analysis and research pack* reflects the policy shift away from income, which was a key indicator under Labour's child poverty strategy, to indicators of worklessness, family breakdown, problem debt and substance misuse. The publication sets out nine national indicators to track progress on tackling disadvantages that affect family and child outcomes. It shows that children in workless families are more likely to experience a larger number of disadvantages that can impact on their longer-term outcomes. A workless family is likely to have between 2 and 2.5 parental disadvantages compared to just over 0.5 for working families in the top 60 per cent of the population. Parental disadvantages include living with: at least one parent reporting a long-standing limiting illness and/or disability; at least one parent reporting poor mental health; both parents having low and/or no qualifications; and in a household reporting signs of problem debt.

ACEs are a set of stressful events experienced in childhood that are associated with the greater incidence of poor physical and mental health, as well as the chances of anti-social behaviour as an adult (Bellis et al, 2014). ACEs include: domestic violence; parental abandonment through separation or divorce; a parent with a mental health condition; being the victim of abuse (physical, sexual and/or emotional); being the victim of neglect (physical and emotional); having a member of the household who is in prison; and growing up in a household in which there are adults experiencing alcohol and drug use problems. A Welsh retrospective survey found that adults who had four or more ACEs as children are more likely to be in prison, develop heart disease, develop type 2 diabetes, have committed violence in the last 12 months and/or engage in high-risk drinking or drug use compared with those adults who had no ACEs (Bellis et al, 2015). A number of public agencies, such as Public Health Scotland, are using information about ACEs as screening tools. The focus on ACEs has provided an important impetus for public policy and services to understand how difficult or traumatic experiences in childhood can have long-lasting effects into adulthood. However, there are some dangers in this approach; ACEs focus on risks and not on protective factors; they are retrospective; and the impact of ACEs will vary between individuals. Importantly, they are not a predictive tool, though they are sometimes being used as such (Early Intervention Foundation, 2018).

The fourth approach undertaken by the Office of the Children's Commissioner in England in 2018 is a framework to understand and quantify childhood vulnerability and the extent to which government recognises and addresses multiple vulnerability through the services that it finances or provides. The vulnerability framework is based on 37 types of childhood risk factors. It finds that there are 2.1 million children in England living with substantial complex needs and that three quarters of these have no recognised form of additional support (Children's Commissioner for England, 2018). The analysis draws on data sets and surveys, and tells us about aggregate levels of risk and vulnerability; it cannot tell us about individual children or families. This framework includes risks not identified in the frameworks described earlier: children with unresolved immigration status; children who may be unsure of their sexual identity; and children at risk of forced marriage. Hence, the numbers in this framework are considerably higher than previous efforts to quantify vulnerable children. The framework aims to fulfil a key role for the Children's Commissioner in England, which is to protect the rights of all children, especially the most vulnerable.

Each framework emphasises different factors, which reflects their purpose and the political context in which they were developed. The SETF framework includes low income as a risk factor; by contrast, the DWP framework is focused on worklessness and other associated parental disadvantages, such as problem debt. The ACEs approach differs from the other frameworks in that it relies on adults reflecting on their past experiences rather than current data about children's and families' lives. However, their findings are corroborated by other studies that track children and adults over their life course. The ACEs do not include worklessness or poverty as a childhood factor that may lead to poor outcomes.

These approaches expose ideological biases when looking for policy solutions. The ACEs approach is focused on behavioural factors and mental health rather than systems failures. The DWP framework combines an emphasis on worklessness and parental behaviours. This focus on worklessness has diverted attention from in-work poverty, which has grown significantly over the period. All the frameworks are useful in planning services and understanding the scale of need in a community. However, none take account of the dynamic nature of poverty. They can and have been used by some to blame individuals rather than to look for wider contextual and structural failures. As we argue throughout this book, it is vital to look both at the system factors that increase pressures for families and at supporting the development of parental and children's capabilities.

It is important to remember that some of the most disadvantaged children are missing from social statistics on child poverty and multidimensional disadvantage, such as those living in residential care. To help rectify this, the Centre for the Analysis of Social Exclusion (CASE) undertook a study to look at 'invisible' or missing children, focusing on Roma, Gypsy and Traveller children, children in recent migrant families, young carers, and children at risk of abuse and neglect (Burchardt et al, 2018). It is critical to be able to document the number and experience of these children both to enable a full picture of all children's needs, including the most vulnerable, and if we are to galvanise action by governments and others to address their needs.

These different ways of measuring and understanding how poverty and other disadvantages combine throw into sharp relief those families with intense, complex and often entrenched difficulties that profoundly shape their children's experiences and life chances. However, children who face multiple and overlapping deprivation or ACEs are a relatively small proportion of all children in poverty. It is therefore important to distinguish between different definitions: those children in poverty; those in persistent poverty; and those facing multiple deprivation. Each will have differing impacts on children's lives and futures and therefore require different policy responses. Policy also needs to take account of the dynamic nature of family life. While highly tailored and sustained public services, alongside family and community support, are the right responses to tackle deep, persistent and multiple problems for a minority of poor families, there is equally a need for policies that reach the wider group of children and families who are in or at risk of poverty.

Conclusion

It is clear that poor child outcomes are the result of a complex interplay between socio-economic conditions, parental resources (finances, social class and education) and a range of intermediate factors that influence the child's immediate environment. Inequalities in child outcomes are manifest early on in a child's life and often persist through childhood and adolescence, shaping later adult outcomes. Despite these patterns of disadvantage, there is great potential to improve the life chances of all children. There is differing evidence for the relative importance of parents' income, SES and educational background, as well as the HLE. However, each clearly matters to child outcomes. Family instability and separation are also closely linked to poverty and deprivation, but they have an independent impact on some child outcomes. To have maximum impact, policies, services and interventions need to be holistic, addressing socio-economic factors alongside family factors such as maternal mental health, couple and parenting support, and good-quality early years services – reducing pressures and increasing capabilities. They also need to address difficulties early on in a child's life, but also throughout childhood, adolescence and the transition to adulthood. The evidence used here has had a significant role in shaping public policy. In Chapter Four, we explore what successive governments have tried to do to level the playing field between poor children and their better-off peers.

Notes

[1] RCTs are the most rigorous way of determining whether a cause–effect relation exists between an intervention and outcome. RCTs are studies in which a number of similar people are randomly assigned to two (or more) groups to test a specific intervention. One group (the experimental group) has the intervention being tested; the other (the comparison or control group) has no intervention. The groups are followed up to see how effective the experimental intervention was.

[2] QEDs are studies used to estimate the causal impact of an intervention on its target population without random assignment. They include observational studies of changes over time.

[3] For academic debate about some methodological issues in the original analysis and the difficulties of measuring children's cognitive skills consistently at different ages, see Feinstein (2015b).

[4] See: www.eif.org.uk/blog/childrens-development-and-family-circumstances-exploring-the-seed-data

[5] When this research was undertaken, the latest MCS sweep of data was age 11.

[6] See: https://cls.ucl.ac.uk/poor-mental-health-is-more-prevalent-among-teenage-girls-from-poorer-backgrounds-new-findings-show/

[7] See: www.nytimes.com/2019/02/07/opinion/helicopter-parents-economy.html

[8] 'Locus of control' refers to the beliefs a person holds about what causes their experiences and to what to attribute success or failure. Someone who attributes their success to luck or fate has an external locus of control; someone who attributes it to their own efforts or motivation has an internal locus of control.

[9] Radio 4 Analysis, 'Do children of married parents do better?', 10 February 2019, available at: www.bbc.co.uk/programmes/m0002b9z

[10] Note that Gordon et al (2016) find slightly differing impacts of inter-parental conflict on child mental health by gender than Fitzsimons and Villadsen (2018), who focus on the impact of separation on child mental health (see p.50).

[11] Specifically, how many days a week the child has breakfast and how many portions of fruit per day.

FOUR

THE ROLE OF GOVERNMENT: A CHANGING PICTURE

This chapter explores how family policies over the last two decades have attempted to improve children's outcomes. It gives an account of how government policy has been crafted in response to research evidence, as well as public opinion and political ideologies. While each political administration brings differences of outlook, we also see differences of emphasis *within* administrations, as well as continuities *between* administrations. The research described in Chapter Three has been used and sometimes misused to devise approaches to improve the outcomes of poor children. Policies were designed to either reduce pressures on families or build capabilities, or sometimes both. In Chapter Five, we assess the success of those policies.

The election of Labour in 1997 marked the end of a long period of Conservative rule, during which conventional attitudes about the family and the role of mothers in the family held sway. It is important to reflect briefly on the social attitudes prevalent before the 1997 election, if only to understand the scale of the changes to come. The 1992 Conservative manifesto was almost silent on parents and families. The private and voluntary sector provision of childcare was seen as a key strength in the British system; early education was noticeably absent; and childcare was contained within the section on women and diversity, reflecting the view that this was a woman's responsibility. While hardship facing lone mothers was of concern, in keeping with public views on mothers' employment, the Conservative government prioritised chasing absent fathers for child support rather than encouraging female workforce participation. The Child Support Agency was set up in 1993 to ensure that fathers paid child maintenance, which was an indication that the state did have a role in family policy, particularly if failing to chase fathers meant more demand on the welfare system for lone mothers and the children left behind. It enforced parental responsibility for both parents, signalling that fathers were a key part of family policy, albeit focused primarily on their financial responsibilities rather than a wider view of their role.

Policy was neutral in relation to mothers' participation in paid work. While there were commitments to tax breaks for childcare, no new childcare provision was promised. Indeed, the introduction of a voucher scheme for childcare in 1996 was designed to give parents greater choice in the voluntary and private markets of childcare. It was assumed by the government of the day that parental demand would drive up quantity and parental choice would drive up quality. Conservative governments had also rejected attempts to define poverty. On 11 May 1989, John Moore, then Secretary of State for Social Security, in his famous 'end of the line for poverty' speech, argued that absolute poverty no longer existed and that relative poverty was, in fact, inequality. Families were described as being on 'low incomes' rather than being in poverty. At this point, the Conservatives believed that the role of the state was limited to what was set out in the Children Act 1989: the state should intervene only when failure to do so could lead to significant harm to the child. Local authorities had a duty to identify *children in need* and provide additional social work support so that children at risk of seriously poor outcomes would not be taken into state care. As late as 1997, John Major's foreword to the Conservative Party manifesto was explicit about aiming to *minimise unnecessary interference in family life* (Conservative Party, 1997).

However, there were some glimmers of change that paved the way for New Labour's family policies. There was a greater interest in the equal opportunities agenda, in particular, from large employers. In 1992, Opportunity 2000 was set up by Business in the Community, chaired by Lady Howe with the backing of the Prime Minister John Major. Its goal was to improve the representation of women at the top of business and public institutions. Gillian Shepherd's influence at the Department of Education helped catalyse the early years agenda; in addition to the childcare voucher, there was a £220 million investment from the National Lottery in the Out-of-School Initiative, which aimed to create out-of-school childcare places for 865,000 children across the UK by 2003. Despite the UK's opt-out from the social chapter of the Maastricht Treaty, its ratification and the creation of the European Union in 1993 marked a shift in social policy horizons.

New Labour and active family policy, 1997–2010

Laying the foundations

The landslide Labour victory in 1997 signalled a much more interventionist approach on a wide range of social policies, most of which had some relationship to family policy: education, early childhood, youth crime, childcare, health and employment. The Institute for Public Policy Research (IPPR), a left-leaning think tank, had been instrumental in developing New Labour's policy programme. Following Labour's 1992 defeat, attributed to its 'tax and spend' package, the Commission on Social Justice was set up to develop an ambitious economic and social reform agenda by the then Labour leader John Smith. *Social justice, strategies for national renewal* (Commission on Social Justice/IPPR, 1994) argued that social justice and economic success went hand in hand. The deregulators of the Thatcher era and the levellers of old Labour were rejected in favour of an investment state. This meant a radical expansion of education, from universal early years provision to lifelong learning; a jobs, training and education strategy to reach the long-term unemployed and lone parents; a National Minimum Wage; and what was described as a social revolution in women's life chances at work and at home.

Labour had to prove its credentials in relation to the management of the economy and so had accepted the previous Conservative public spending plans for the first two years in government, freezing lone-parent benefit and increasing the pension by a paltry 5p. Both were heavily criticised. The creation of the Prime Minister's Strategy Unit right at the heart of government emphasised the use of evidence and analysis of social issues to design clearer roles for the state and for policy development. Labour had inherited a growing economy, which became more buoyant during most of its term in office, with growing tax revenues until the global financial crash of 2008. The combination of a strong economy and large parliamentary majority enabled its social programme to be financed with little recourse to increases in taxation or borrowing, or a pressing need to make a public case for redistribution.

The shift in attitudes to women working and the powerful voice of the largest number of women MPs ever elected to the House of Commons helped to propel gender equality up the political agenda. The Labour Party manifesto of 1997 (Labour Party, 1997) promised a comprehensive childcare strategy that would enable more mothers to work. Labour's policy on childcare was meant to achieve three key policy goals: improvements in equality of opportunity for women; a reduction in child poverty; and an improvement in educational outcomes through the provision of universal free early education for four year olds. Successive governments have grappled with the tensions between these three goals. For labour market participation, childcare has to be affordable and flexible. To improve life chances for children, particularly those from low-income families, early education has to be high in quality and delivered with regularity and consistency. While governments across the period have increased their investment in early years provision, the funding has largely gone on expanding free hours for three, four and some two year olds rather than improving the qualifications and pay of the workforce, which are key factors in building quality. This stemmed from the predominance of the Treasury view that the primary purpose of expanding childcare was enabling women to enter the labour market. Policies were focused on stimulating the demand for childcare through childcare tax credits for low-income families rather than boosting the supply of childcare through direct state provision. Ministers have limited time in office and want to demonstrate achievements. A factor in deciding which of the three goals is most important may relate to the time it takes to know if the policy is achieving the goal. Assessing the impact of the increased availability and affordability of childcare on labour market participation is relatively easy to measure over the lifetime of a Parliament. Knowing if improvements in the quality of early education and childcare have positive impacts on the life chances of children is harder to measure and takes much longer to establish.

Although efforts have been made to ensure that policy is responsive to all three goals, party-political priorities have shifted over time, as have the priorities within and across government departments. In 2001, the Department for Work and Pensions (DWP) was created, taking over the employment responsibilities of what was the Department for Education and Employment (DfEE). During negotiations on which responsibilities would go to the new department, there was a proposal that childcare should come out of the DfEE (renamed the Department for Education and Skills [DfES]) and move to the DWP. This was resisted but demonstrates how strong the view was that the goal of female labour market participation could not be met without adequate childcare. Given the evidence in Chapter Three about the direct relationship between poverty and poor outcomes for children, employment was reasonably seen as a clear route to reducing child poverty *and* improving child outcomes.

New Labour was also interested in wider family policy issues beyond early years provision. The then Home Secretary, Jack Straw, also had responsibility for family policy. *Supporting families* (Home Office, 1998) was the new government's first attempt to set out its views on the importance of strengthening family life. It recognised ongoing changes in family patterns while trying not to preach to families. Three principles were established: the paramount interests of children in order to ensure that the next generation had the best start in life; children's need for stability and security, with marriage as the *surest foundation for raising children*; and support for all parents to enable them to support their children. A National Family and Parenting Institute and new national parenting helpline were established. Labour's policy trod a fine line between supporting marriage and not stigmatising unmarried couples and lone-parent families. While the *family* was the focus in the Home Office, the DfES and the Treasury had a stronger emphasis on the child. In practice, policies were primarily directed towards children, sidestepping the issue of family structure. A small but significant acknowledgement of the rise of cohabitating parents was a legal change in 2003 that enabled unmarried fathers to acquire legal parental responsibility if they were registered as the child's father on the birth certificate. This was also an important recognition of a father's role that extended beyond financial responsibilities. The liberalisation of attitudes to diverse families and sexuality that we documented in Chapter Two helped pave the way for the 2004 civil partnership legislation, which enabled same-sex couples to have very similar rights and responsibilities as opposite-sex couples married in a civil ceremony. This included property, benefit and pension rights, as well as the right to parental responsibility for a partner's children.

Family policy was also influenced by the government's pro-European agenda; the UK signed up to a series of European Union directives on parental leave, working time and equality at work. Scandinavia was seen as the model for progressive countries; it had generous maternity and paternity leave arrangements and highly developed childcare provision. Working towards these standards, but never achieving them, the 2001 Labour Party manifesto (Labour Party, 2001) promised the extension of paid maternity leave from 11 weeks to six months, at a rate of £100 per week. The same manifesto also promised the provision of free part-time nursery education for all three year olds.

Along with childcare and early education for young children, the Labour government was deeply concerned with child poverty in its first two terms. Indeed, in 1999, Tony Blair announced his aim to eradicate child poverty in two decades. Gordon Brown, in his role as Chancellor of the Exchequer, led on the New Deal, which focused on tackling unemployment and incentivising work through increasing work obligations, the National Minimum Wage and tax credits. All these policies channelled financial support to families both in and out of work. The focus on child poverty was later embodied in a set of targets and entrenched across government departments. *Rights and responsibilities* were a key feature of the approach: on one side, tax credits and lower childcare costs; on the other, increased obligations on claimants to search for work, combined with support with training and work preparation. The very big increase in employment for lone parents and the reduction in child poverty during the period show that the combined strategy had the desired effect (see Chapter Five).

Labour was also interested in reducing the negative impacts of poverty on children so that the next generation would not be poor. Educational reform was a major part of these efforts, along with an emphasis on integrated, joined-up family services and parent support. The most well known of these initiatives was

Sure Start, announced in Parliament in 1998 and initially aimed at all families with children under four years old in particularly poor neighbourhoods (Eisenstadt, 2011). Sure Start drew on an extensive body of international evidence and was supported by a growing call from early years organisations for much-needed change. Driven from the Treasury by the inspirational and powerful civil servant Norman Glass, this area-based approach was intended to avoid the stigma of targeted services while ensuring that low-income families, who were likely to need the services most, could benefit from them. From the beginning of Sure Start, a key feature was the involvement of local parents in the governance of the programmes, identifying particular needs in the area and what services should be offered, and recruiting staff.

While Sure Start was aimed specifically at families with young children living in poor areas, the Children's Fund was set up in 2000 to help local organisations run support programmes for vulnerable children, aged eight to 13. A Children and Young People's Unit (CYPU) was created to administer the Children's Fund and coordinate family policy across Whitehall. It was a tall order. Disbanded in 2004 as part of the Every Child Matters (ECM) reforms described later, its funding stream for voluntary organisations was absorbed into other parts of the DfES. While the Children's Fund itself did not have a lasting impact, the CYPU did much of the groundwork for ECM.

The Connexions service, an additional strand, was aimed at all young people aged 13 to 19. While it was offered as a universal service, the main aim of Connexions was to reduce the then large numbers of young people over 16 who were not in education, employment or training. Again, while a universal service, the young people most likely to benefit from the Connexions service were from lower-income families. Funding settlements for these three programmes added up to a huge investment in children: in 2002/03, the Sure Start budget was £211 million, the Children's Fund was £149 million and the Connexions service was £441 million (Sefton, 2004).

Alongside new service initiatives, the Labour government continued to work on income transfers. The Educational Maintenance Allowance was introduced in 2004 to provide financial support directly to young people living in families on low incomes in order to enable them to stay on at school or college after the age of 16.

In keeping with New Labour's endeavours on *joined-up* government, these initiatives – Sure Start, the Children's Fund and Connexions – had their own cross-departmental ministerial groups to oversee their progress. Breaking down departmental silos was an innovative approach closely associated with the Blair government's efforts to *modernise government*, not just new policies, but new ways of creating and managing policy across Whitehall on cross-cutting themes.[1]

Policy on parenting extended into the youth justice arena. Early in its first term, the Labour government introduced Parenting Orders. This legislation created a way of making parents accountable for the offending of their children while, at the same time, giving them the support necessary to take proper care of and control over them. Rights and responsibilities were being applied to the social sphere. A Parenting Order is made by the courts and imposes a requirement that the parents or guardians attend counselling or guidance sessions for up to six months, where they receive support in dealing with their children.[2] While there was initial concern about the coercive nature of Parenting Orders, they proved both popular with parents and effective. One major complaint from parents was why support was not offered before things got so bad.[3]

New Labour was designing far-reaching policies to support families with young children, school-aged children and young adults. However, the diversity and complexity of these new initiatives were becoming burdensome on top-tier local authorities and health services, which had to oversee the delivery of a large number of what were separately managed and governed Whitehall directives, all with separate funding streams. For families, access to both targeted and mainstream services was becoming increasingly complex, particularly if a family had more than two children of varying ages. Alongside this, the murder of Victoria Climbie in February 2000 exposed serious failings in child protection and sent shockwaves through the system. She was known to four London boroughs, two hospitals, the police and the National Society for the Prevention of Cruelty to Children (NSPCC). The Lord Laming inquiry that followed identified 12 times when her life could have been saved. Lord Laming's recommendations for a radical overhaul of children's social services fed into a major system reform to bring all aspects of children's lives into one overarching model: ECM.

From piecemeal initiatives to an overall strategy: Every Child Matters

The *Every child matters* Green Paper (DfES, 2003), set out a series of reforms at local government level, establishing five core outcomes that all children should achieve: stay safe; stay healthy; enjoy and achieve; economic well-being; and make a positive contribution. ECM legislation required all local authorities to have a Director of Children's Services, including education and social care, and a lead elected member for children. The key principle of the reforms was the need to ensure individual accountability for all children's outcomes in a locality, rather than accountability through individual services like education, social care or health. Service integration around the needs of the child and family, rather than individual interventions based on professional boundaries, became a key goal.

ECM also drove a major reorganisation of responsibilities at central government level: children's social care was split off from adult social care and moved from the Department of Health to the DfES. The intention was to have all policies concerning children within one Whitehall department and one minister representing them. Moving from an *education* department to a *children's* department was reinforced by Ed Balls when he became Secretary of State in 2007. The DfES became the Department for Children, Schools and Families (DCSF).

The Green Paper also proposed the creation of an independent Children's Commissioner to act as a voice for children and young people, especially disadvantaged children. This was a welcome emphasis on the importance of children and young people's own views as a key part of policymaking. The Children's Commissioners in England, Scotland, Wales and Northern Ireland have been maintained by subsequent administrations.

ECM is a prime example of the extent to which Whitehall was taking control of and dictating to local government on key policy areas that would have previously been entirely up to local discretion. This centralisation of power had been a key feature of the Thatcher years, and it continued under Labour in its first two terms. The public were dissatisfied with postcode lotteries on services, and ministers were keen to demonstrate improvements over relatively short periods of time. If all local authorities were working within the same framework, collecting data and comparing performance became much more transparent. However, there are inherent risks to this approach. Ministers could no longer absolve themselves of responsibility for things going wrong at the local level. The more the press and the public blamed the government for operational failures at the local level, the more governments of all parties sought to take tighter control. A further risk of centralisation is its potential to curb local innovation; it can help to prevent the worst things from happening but also curb the best.

The ECM reforms were largely about integrated approaches to family support, with different agencies working together, sharing information and coming to a coordinated plan for the child and family. Increasingly, this became based on the identification of risks associated with poor child outcomes. Such risks ranged from signs of abuse or neglect, disability, mental health problems, long-term worklessness, poor housing, and poverty itself (for various risk frameworks, see Chapter Three). As described later, in order to appropriately intervene early to prevent further risk escalation, interagency collaboration is crucial.

Alongside ECM, in 2004, the Labour government carried out a major review of early years services, including Sure Start, early education and childcare. The resulting publication, *Choice for parents, the best start for children* (HMT, 2004), set out for the first time in a single document benefit reforms alongside expanded services: increased paid maternity leave from six to nine months, with an entitlement to a year off work; increased paid paternity leave to two weeks; and a right to flexible working for parents with a child up to the age of six (later extended to older children and carers). The improvements in maternity and paternity leave entitlements addressed concerns about group care for children aged under one, taking into account some evidence that long hours in out-of-home care for babies was associated with behavioural problems in school (Belsky, 2001). More recently, the research on early brain development described in Chapter Three has also emphasised the importance of one-to-one care in the first 12 months of life. Aside from financial support through childcare tax credits, little attention was paid to how to support care for babies in their second year.

Politicians were keen to build on the popularity of Sure Start and create a new plank of the welfare state; hence, *Choice for parents* (HMT, 2004) also promised a Sure Start Children's Centre for every neighbourhood, not just poor areas, and all schools would offer extended hours for after-school care. The document and the reforms it ushered in were a step change in the rights and services for parents and children.

There were two further policy initiatives concerning children and family services under New Labour: the Respect Agenda in 2006 (Respect Task Force, 2006) and *Think family: Improving the life chances of families at risk* in 2008 (SETF, 2008). Both of these reports came out of a special unit set up in the Cabinet Office, the Social Exclusion Task Force (SETF). The SETF was a successor to the Social Exclusion Unit, set up at the very beginning of the Labour government in 1997. Having produced a variety of highly influential reports, including on rough sleeping, teen pregnancy and school exclusions, it lost its influence when it was moved to the Department of Communities and Local Government. In 2006, it returned to the Cabinet Office, was slimmed down and was renamed as a *task force*. The role of the SETF was to find cross-government solutions to intractable problems that directly affected only a relatively small number of people but resulted in very high costs to the taxpayer.

The Respect Agenda was a response to continued concern about youth petty crime and was designed to address anti-social behaviour, which was often perpetrated by a handful of families on any estate but could make life a misery for everyone else living in the area. Like the earlier initiative of Parenting Orders, the Respect Agenda took a whole-family approach to preventing a range of behaviours that might be included in an attempt to stop minor offences developing into more serious criminality: playing loud music at unsociable hours; graffiti; offensive and threatening remarks; dumping rubbish; and harassment and intimidation. Policymakers identified the root causes of such behaviours as poor parenting, schools that do not challenge poor behaviour, living in deprived areas and drug and alcohol misuse. Hence, the offer under the Respect Agenda banner was a combination of targeted parenting support, the increased use of Parenting Orders and legislation for greater powers for the police to tackle antisocial behaviour:

Parenting is one of the most important responsibilities in creating a strong society based on mutual respect. Parenting is primarily the business of parents and the Government does not want to interfere with that principle.

But where parents are unwilling, or unable to meet their responsibilities we must ensure that they are challenged and supported to do so. (Respect Task Force, 2006)

The foundations of the Conservatives' Troubled Families programme are to be found in the Respect Agenda, which included the establishment of a pilot programme of Family Intervention Projects (FIPs), working particularly with families involved in anti-social behaviour severe enough to risk eviction from social housing. The approach involved an assessment of the needs of each family member and an agreement of appropriate support in exchange for a commitment to improved behaviours.

Think family (SETF, 2008) aimed to ensure that the support provided by children's, adults' and family services was coordinated and focused on problems affecting the whole family, particularly for those experiencing the most significant risks. The principles of the *Respect action plan* (Respect Task Force, 2006), FIPs and *Think family* (SETF, 2008) are not dissimilar from the ECM agenda, albeit with a highly targeted approach based on certain behaviours and risk factors. It was recognised that strategies to reduce poverty on their own would not solve more entrenched issues, such as anti-social behaviour, and particularly risky behaviours among members of the same family, which require multi-agency and multidisciplinary responses. Adult and child mental health services, education and housing, social services, and the police all had a role to play. However, establishing protocols of joint working and information sharing was, and continues to be, very challenging.

Increasing capabilities: prevention and early intervention

All of the aforementioned policy initiatives rest on a notion of working with children and families on a wide spectrum of need while trying to ensure that family difficulties reduce rather than escalate. Escalating problems are harder to remedy and incur higher costs in the long run. Prevention and early intervention have been features of government policy across administrations, being started under Labour and continued by the Coalition and Conservative governments. There are two ways of looking at these concepts: preventing problems before they become entrenched during any stage of development; or preventing problems by giving children a good start in life, that is, a focus on the early years. Prevention and early intervention can operate at a universal level for all children and families or be targeted on the basis of identified risk factors (Axford and Berry, 2018). The use of evidence-based programmes to support parenting, relationships, the early years and maternal mental health has been strongly associated with early intervention (see Chapter Five).

Two important papers were published in 2007: the *Policy review of children and young people* (HMT and DfES, 2007), which majored on prevention and early intervention; and *Every parent matters* (DfES, 2007). They heralded a new emphasis on and investment in a range of policies on the role of parents and the early years to improve children's life chances. The review by Her Majesty's Treasury (HMT and DfES) argued that preventing problems arising, or, indeed, intervening as soon as they are identified, is essential to maximising children's life chances. Problems could arise at any stage during childhood, and there was a dynamic process where children came in and out of risk. Among the recommendations in the review was an emphasis on the crucial role of universal public services and the role of parents:

> The framework in which public services operate could place more emphasis than it does currently on rewarding or incentivising support which is preventative;…

> parents and communities are vital to create a supportive environment in which children and young people can develop. More can be done to build their capacity to fulfil this role. (HMT and DfES, 2007)

This report promotes the dual approach of tax credits and employment as a means to improve family prosperity alongside service-led parenting support, simultaneously reducing the numbers of children living in poverty while ameliorating the likely impact of less-than-optimal parenting. The review also implies that this dual approach will narrow the gap in outcomes between poor children and their better-off peers. It further argues that intervening early could achieve great cost savings in the future by preventing problems becoming more serious and intractable.

Following the joint HMT/DfES review, the DfES (2007) published *Every parent matters*. This document picked up many of the themes in the HMT/DfES review, emphasising the importance of parents in children's early years, school life and beyond. Taking a life-cycle approach, it describes a range of services aimed at parents that should be available through childhood from perinatal health services, Sure Start children's centres and schools. Crucially, it provides examples of support services that should be available across the spectrum of need, from universal offers to specialist services for deeply entrenched problems. The National Academy for Parenting Practitioners (NAPP) was set up at Kings College in 2007 to train and support the practitioners that parents would turn to for advice. The Parenting Early Intervention Programme was set up and ran between 2008 and 2011, providing funding to all local authorities to offer one or more of five evidenced-based parenting programmes. Labour also piloted what became known as Family Nurse Partnerships, an intensive attachment-based programme for teenage mothers, described in more detail in Chapter Five.

In 2007, Gordon Brown took over as Labour leader and Prime Minister. When the global financial crisis hit in 2008, his response was a fiscal stimulus both to boost the economy and to support vulnerable groups through the downturn (HMT, 2009). The Budget of that year brought in the largest increase in child tax credits since 2004, as well as other benefit improvements for families (Stewart and Obolenskaya, 2016). Under Brown's aegis, ending child poverty was entrenched in legislation, the Child Poverty Act 2010. The Act set statutory targets for the reduction of child poverty and a requirement for government to report annually on progress towards the targets. It was enacted during the end of the Brown years, with the hope that by setting the goal of ending child poverty into a legal framework, it would be harder to undo (for the four different measures of poverty, see Box 4.1).

BOX 4.1 CHILD POVERTY TARGETS

- Relative poverty – to reduce the proportion of children who live in relative low income (in families with incomes below 60 per cent of the median, before housing costs) to less than 10 per cent.
- Combined low income and material deprivation – to reduce the proportion of children who live in material deprivation and have a low income (below 70 per cent of the median, before housing costs) to less than 5 per cent.
- Persistent poverty – to reduce the proportion of children that experience long periods of relative poverty, with the specific target to be set by December 2014.
- Absolute poverty – to reduce the proportion of children who live below an income threshold fixed in real terms to less than 5 per cent.

Source: HMG (2010)

Just before the general election in 2010, the DCSF (2010) published *Support for all: The families and relationships Green Paper* under the leadership of Ed Balls, then Secretary of State at the DCSF. It is significant in highlighting the importance of family relationships and makes recommendations to provide support for relationship counselling, mediation and parenting support for separating couples. This policy theme was then to feature more strongly under the Coalition and Conservatives.

The Labour years were characterised by substantial investment in children and families, with a vast array of policies on benefits and tax credits, as well as services. Over the period, universal free education was expanded, from children aged five to 16, to children aged three to 18. Blair strongly believed that public services had to be so good that there would be no incentive to seek private health care or education. He believed that a willingness to pay taxes was dependent on the quality available for all. There was an activist family policy at work, characterised by a dual strategy of both reducing pressures and building the capabilities of families and children. However, within the Labour government, there were different views on priorities. As illustrated in the debates on childcare, the Treasury and the DWP were most interested in reducing poverty by getting mothers into the labour market. Blair was most interested in reducing the likelihood of poverty for the future generation by improving educational attainment, as well as narrowing the gap in attainment between poor children and their better-off peers. Matching rights with responsibilities was a key feature of the reforms for both Brown and Blair. Policies encompassed all children, not just those in poverty, what Gordon Brown termed *progressive universalism*. In their last term in office, both Blair and Brown increasingly focused on families with complex problems in recognition of the fact that broader policies had failed to reach the small number of families with multiple difficulties. They took a mixed approach, from encouraging local design and local solutions, to increasingly dictating from Whitehall what had to be done with different funding streams and a variety of reporting arrangements. The ECM agenda was a comprehensive effort to pull all these streams together, but it had little time to really embed locally before the government changed and new approaches were started.

The financial crisis of 2008 and the subsequent recession led to a huge increase in government borrowing following 2008 as the gap between public sector spending and tax revenues widened to an extent not seen since the Second World War. Labour's response was a fiscal stimulus to mitigate the impact of the recession and maintain social programmes in order to protect the poorest. In the run-up to the 2010 general election, all the political parties put forward substantial fiscal tightening (Chote et al, 2010). The main difference between their approaches was the pace at which they proposed to address the debt and the balance between public spending cuts and tax rises. Labour proposed a 2:1 ratio of spending cuts to tax rises, the Liberal Democrats 2.5:1 and the Conservatives 4:1.

Labour's overall record was overshadowed by the fallout from the global financial crash. The lack of regulation of the City and the financial sector was widely recognised as a key driver of the crisis. However, a political narrative developed following the crisis that blamed the growing deficit on profligate spending during the boom years under Labour, a failure to *repair the roof while the sun was shining*. In fact, the budget deficit and level of debt grew from 2008 largely as a result of the recession, which saw a sharp rise in unemployment and a collapse of tax revenue. However, the strength of the narrative on profligacy gave the incoming Coalition government carte blanche to dramatically cut both services and benefits.

Family policy under the Coalition government

The Coalition government under David Cameron took a very different view of family policy from that of his Conservative prime ministerial predecessors, Thatcher and Major. Working with the Liberal Democrats, a number of new policies and commitments on improving social mobility were evident early on, symbolised by the Deputy Prime Minister Nick Clegg's announcement of a Commission on Child Poverty and Social Mobility, headed by the former Labour minister Alan Milburn. Notably, this marked a shift in emphasis from child poverty to social mobility, and with it, a focus on services rather than income measures. The Coalition also made an ongoing commitment to the National Minimum Wage. However, the central element of the Coalition Agreement hammered out between the Liberal Democrats and the Conservatives was the commitment to eliminating the deficit over the lifetime of the Parliament at a faster rate than had been forecast in Labour's last Budget. Three quarters of that reduction was to be achieved through public spending cuts and a quarter through tax rises. This left the government with very little wriggle room in terms of new spending and a huge amount of political capital invested in austerity. The key demographic group for the Conservatives was clearly pensioners, who were protected from spending cuts (alongside schools and health); pensioners were promised a triple lock on protected increases in the state pension, as well as continued free winter fuel allowances and free bus travel. All taxpayers were to benefit from rises in the personal tax allowance – an expensive policy at a time of severely constrained finances. Meanwhile, poorer single working-aged adults and families with children had their cash benefits initially protected for the first two years of the Coalition government but were in line to face severe benefits cuts from 2013 onwards.

The Coalition government continued the commitment to applying evidence to policy but shifted its emphasis. The Behavioural Insights Team, heavily influenced by 'nudge economics', put behavioural science at the heart of the government's policymaking. The essence of this approach is that a small change – 'a nudge' – for example, in the way a message is framed or through an opt-out rather than opt-in policy, can sometimes enable people to make the 'right' choices.[4] These ideas had started to filter through under the previous administration but grew in influence after 2010. This greater emphasis on the insights from behavioural psychology was politically helpful at a time of very constrained resources as it focuses on small low-cost changes to influence behaviour rather than addressing wider systems failures.

Setting the tone: Breakdown Britain

The shift in Conservative thinking on family policy and particularly on parenting can be traced back to 2006, when the Centre for Social Justice (CSJ) published its report *Breakdown Britain* (Social Justice Policy Group, 2006). The report had been commissioned by David Cameron as leader of the opposition. The CSJ, a centre-right think tank, was set up in 2004 by Iain Duncan Smith, a former leader of the Conservatives, to offer a contrasting view on solving social problems. He argued that social issues, in particular, addressing poverty, were important for Conservatives but that the Labour approach was fundamentally flawed. The report argued that Labour's policies had focused on a single income threshold, did not give due attention to worklessness and had led to a substantial increase in means testing (for a discussion of these issues, see Chapter Five). Instead, *Breakdown Britain* focused on five pathways to poverty: family breakdown, educational failure, economic dependence, indebtedness and addiction. As is well known from Marmot (2010), Wilkinson and Pickett (2009) and many others, there is a strong correlation between poverty and the five issues identified. However, describing a 'pathway' to poverty implies a one-way cause and effect relationship rather than a set of complex correlations (see Chapter Three). The CSJ report emphasised the importance of fathers in children's lives and the intergenerational risks of families headed up by lone mothers. *Breakdown Britain* often refers to the negative behaviours of parents being repeated by their offspring, as well as the importance of marriage and stable relationships to child outcomes. The basic premise of the report is that economic dependency and educational failure, alongside problematic behaviours in adults, drive poor outcomes for children. These poor outcomes set up intergenerational disadvantage. However, it fails to mention that lack of income itself has a relationship with poor outcomes for children. As research described in Chapter Three confirms, in many practical ways, it is harder to be a 'good' parent with limited income. While families suffering from a range of disadvantages are more likely to be poor, most families in poverty do not have complex problems brought on by their own behaviour. They simply lack the resources to provide their children with the goods and experiences that can protect against poor outcomes.

Breakdown Britain provided a rationale about social policy that would be specifically targeted at those most in need and built around the five identified drivers of poverty. Central to the vision was creating a 'Welfare Society', with the family and voluntary and community sector as the best means of delivering the support necessary to address the drivers of poverty. This approach became a reality when Iain Duncan Smith became the Chair of a newly created Cabinet Committee on Social Justice, as well as being the Secretary of State for the DWP.

The emphasis on the role of the voluntary and community sector was reflected in the Conservative Party manifesto in 2010, which talked about a 'Big Society rather than Big Government.' Symbolic of this approach was the introduction of the National Citizens Service in 2011, a social action programme for young people aged 16 and 17 from all social backgrounds. Most interesting of all was David Cameron's challenge to the Thatcher view that there is no such thing as society. His response was: 'We believe there is such a thing as society – it's just not the same thing as the state' (Cameron, 2007). The Big Society theme was to be short-lived. However, the Conservatives of 2010 were less wary of the nanny state than their 1992 counterparts. Cameron saw a wider role for everyone in raising the next generation, as expressed on the opening page of the 2010 manifesto: 'How will we raise responsible children unless every adult plays their part?' (Conservative Party, 2010). Crucially, it says 'every adult', not just mothers and fathers.

Active family policy constrained by austerity

The Coalition government of 2010 built on the previous government's emphasis on parenting and the early years, extending the Labour pilot on childcare for disadvantaged two year olds from the bottom quintile to the bottom 40 per cent, a Liberal Democrat policy. It also increased the number of health visitors, expanded Family Nurse Partnerships and created an Early Intervention Grant for local authorities to catalyse early intervention. This grant essentially replaced the Sure Start grant, removing a brand highly associated with a flagship programme of the Labour years. The grant stood at £3.2 billion for 2010–11 and brought together different services, ranging from the early years and children's centres, to teenage pregnancy services. By 2015/16, the value of the grant had been more than halved to around £1.4 billion as a result of the substantial reductions imposed by the Coalition government on local authorities (CYPN et al, 2015). Other Labour programmes were dropped altogether. Signalling a re-emphasis on education, the ECM agenda was rapidly dismantled and what was the DCSF became the Department for Education. The Educational Maintenance Allowance was stopped and the Connexions Service was dismantled as a national programme, being replaced by a National Careers Service.

Following the 2010 election, public attitudes had started to shift from opposition to spending cuts to cautious support (Seldon and Snowdon, 2016). The first Coalition Budget ushered in £11 billion of welfare benefit cuts, particularly affecting families. These included reductions in housing benefits, uprating benefits and tax credits by the Consumer Price Index (rather than the usually higher Retail Price Index), freezing child benefit, reducing eligibility to child tax credits, and moving lone parents with children over the age of five onto Job Seekers Allowance, therefore making them available for work.

Additionally, a public sector pay freeze for those earning above £21,000 resulted in substantial changes to the living standards of those on lower earnings. Austerity was forcing reduced spending on services as well as reduced income transfers.

The Coalition government commissioned four reports on children, three of which are of particular relevance here.[5] Labour MP Frank Field (2010) produced *The foundation years: Preventing poor children becoming poor adults*. He suggested an alternative strategy to abolish child poverty – one that shifted away from tackling child poverty through income redistribution to developing poor children's capabilities in the early years. Reflecting much of the material in *Breakdown Britain*, Field argued that parents on low incomes are less likely to have the capabilities to provide the stimulation needed for a good start in life. Their children will therefore be less likely to do well at school, and less likely to achieve academic results that will lead to good jobs. Field recommended that the government stop uprating benefit levels and invest the savings on intensive parenting support and high-quality integrated early years services for the poorest children. His recommendation was very helpful to a government desperate for savings after the financial crisis of 2008. Highly targeted parenting support and early years provision would be significantly less costly than increases in benefits. The two-pronged approach adopted by the previous Labour government – reducing pressures through cash transfers while increasing capabilities with increased investment in parenting support – was beginning to unravel (Stewart and Obolenskaya, 2016).

Another Labour MP, Graham Allen, produced the report *Early intervention: The next steps*.[6] Allen argued that a strategy of early intervention and prevention was not only more effective for enabling children to thrive, but also more economically efficient. The report focused on building *social and emotional capabilities* for babies, children and young people, often neglected by public policy in comparison with cognitive skills. It argued that while the early years were a particularly important period in child development, action was needed throughout childhood and adolescence. Allen's report urged investment in parenting and other *programmes* that had been rigorously tested and shown to deliver results. He wanted to ensure that what little resource was available was spent on interventions that were delivered early enough, were to a high enough standard and had proven effective elsewhere. We discuss some of the opportunities and the challenges in implementing this approach in Chapter Five. The Coalition's recognition of the importance of social and emotional skills built on Labour's Improving Access to Psychological Therapies programme but took it further with the commitment to parity of esteem between mental and physical health, investment in services to support children's mental health, and treatment for post-natal depression.

The third of these influential reviews was *The Munro review of child protection: A child centred system* (Munro, 2011). It focused on the most vulnerable children in the social care system. Among a number of recommendations, it called for a shift from a compliance to a learning culture, the development of social work expertise, and a duty on local authorities and their statutory partners to secure sufficient provision of local 'early help' services for children, young people and families. While local authorities introduced an array of 'early help' measures to work with the most disadvantaged families on the edge of care, the *duty* to provide early help has not been enacted in legislation. The appointment of a Chief Social Worker, Isobel Trowler, in 2013 signified a commitment to reform children's social services, which has now culminated in the creation of a What Works Centre on Children's Social Care. However, the failure to make early help a statutory duty, in combination with sharp reductions in local authority funding and growing rates of looked-after children, has increasingly squeezed out funding for early help and early intervention, leaving many vulnerable families with too little, too late (Family Rights Group, 2018).

Alongside the attempt to improve children's social care was a major reform of the family justice system, catalysed by the Family justice review, (Ministry of Justice, 2011) chaired by David Norgrove. The family justice system deals with families when things have gone seriously wrong, failures of parenting and relationships where anger, domestic violence, abuse, drugs and alcohol are often involved. The review argued that the family justice system did not constitute a system at all; it drew attention to the delays and confusion faced by families and children, complex organisational structures, and the lack of trust and leadership. Many of its recommendations were included in what was a radical piece of legislation, the Children and Families Act 2014. It put children at the heart of the system, creating a Family Justice Young People's Board, a single Family Court, a 26-week limit for care and supervision cases, and a legal requirement to attend a mediation meeting before taking a dispute over children to the court. However, these reforms took place while legal aid for private law cases was sharply reduced, leaving most parents having to represent themselves. How the family courts deal with the consequences of (usually) parental failure remains a key challenge and has led to fundamental policy questions about whether the courts are there to resolve disputes, that is, deal with the symptoms, or solve underlying problems.

Two organisations of particular interest to family and children's policy were set up under the Coalition: the Early Intervention Foundation (EIF) and the Education Endowment Foundation (EEF). They were both What Works Centres, organisations designated by the government to provide expert advice on science and evidence-based approaches to social interventions and policies.

The EIF was set up by Graham Allen after his *Next steps* report was published. It was created to establish the efficacy of various forms of early intervention in children's lives and to support local areas in implementation. The EEF was set up to identify interventions that improve classroom practice in order to help narrow the gap in school outcomes between poor children and their better-off peers.[7] The amount of government funding allocated to each of these organisations is a good indicator of where they set their priorities – education rather than family policy was to win out. The EEF's initial funding was in the order of £125 million. By contrast, the EIF's initial funding from the government was £3.5 million. While the political rhetoric about early intervention and early help was strong, the cumulative reduction in local authority and public health funding after 2010 was to hit this part of the system very hard.

Against the backdrop of austerity, another major investment under the Coalition was the Troubled Families programme. It was established as a response to the 2011 riots. In their wake, the government adapted Labour's earlier FIPs to create a £448 million programme directed at 120,000 families with multiple risks and, in some cases, chaotic lives. The argument was made that £9 billion is spent annually on troubled families, of which £8 billion is spent on reactive spend compared to £1 billion on preventing problems. Funding was directed to local authorities on a payment-by-results basis, with the aim of 'turning around' the lives of the 120,000 by 2015. This is an example of policy continuity between administrations; both had prime ministerial backing and Louise Casey was in charge of the policy for Labour, the Coalition and the Conservatives. However, Troubled Families was pitched with a particularly strong political rhetoric, both to distinguish it from the previous policy and to match public concern about the riots. It also fell into the trap of overstating its achievements (see Chapter Five).

Many of the reforms designed to address family policy under the Coalition government were cost neutral or required little investment. The Coalition government built on Labour's family-friendly policies, with Nick Clegg in the lead. They introduced more flexibility between mothers and fathers on the use of parental leave, which was an important first step in improving the balance of entitlements between women and men.

In keeping with the principles outlined in *Breakdown Britain*, David Cameron reintroduced the Marriage Allowance, which was largely symbolic as it was set at a very low level. He also put funding for relationship support on a more secure footing, which was consistent with the view that married and stable couple families had the best chance of raising healthy children. Surprisingly, David Cameron went a step further than Labour's earlier reforms that brought in civil partnerships for gay couples, and introduced gay marriage. Conservative politicians were keen to see marriage as an important component of good parenting and extended this to parenting by same-sex couples.

A major reform to the welfare system that was not cost neutral was being designed under the leadership of Iain Duncan Smith at the DWP. It drew heavily on a report by the CSJ called *Dynamic benefits* (Economic Dependency Working Group, 2009) and the analysis in *Breakdown Britain*. Duncan Smith's view was that the welfare system was fatally flawed; there were some situations where families were better off out of work than in work, and the system was impossibly complex and difficult to navigate even for advisors. He was keen to develop a system that would provide strong incentives to increase working hours, as well as being simpler for both recipient and advisor to understand. Universal Credit (UC) was designed to combine six means-tested benefits into one monthly payment. It was also meant to ensure that any individual would be better off in work than on out-of-work benefits. However, among the means-tested benefits not included in UC was council tax benefit. As a result, on average, UC benefit recipients in employment are likely to be worse off.[8]

Unfortunately, the new system was dependent on injections of cash in the short term, with promises of savings in the future. The Chancellor, George Osborne, was unwilling to compromise his austerity plans with sufficient funding for the new system. He continued sharp benefits cuts that significantly compromised Duncan Smith's vision for the new system and led to his resignation from the cabinet. At the time of writing, there have been further delays in the roll-out of UC, with a demand from opposition parties and others for the reform to be dropped altogether. As a result, there has been a substantial injection of funding in the 2018 Budget to help reduce the number of households who would be net losers (see Chapter Five).

There continues to be fierce debate on how much influence the Liberal Democrats had on Coalition policies. In terms of family policy, two Liberal Democrat policies stand out and are perfectly divided between reducing pressures and increasing capabilities. The Pupil Premium, ensuring that schools get extra resources for every child eligible for free school meals, did not directly reduce pressures on families, but it did acknowledge the difficulties that schools face in narrowing the gap between poor children and their better-off peers. The Pupil Premium originally applied only to children of statutory school age. It was extended to three and four year olds but at a much reduced rate. Schools receive £1,900 per eligible school-aged child; and early years providers receive £300 for every eligible three and four year old. The Liberal Democrats were also responsible for extending free school meals to all children in infant classes, that is, up to about age eight, which is a policy that both reduces pressures and increases children's capabilities.

By contrast, the Can Parent Initiative championed by Nick Clegg was designed to increase the market for parenting programmes by offering all parents a voucher to attend a parenting programme. By offering the voucher to all parents, it was hoped that the stigma sometimes associated with attending such programmes would be removed. The voucher system was also expected to stimulate the market for parenting programmes. Unsurprisingly, the Pupil Premium proved to be very popular and extensive work has been done through the EEF's toolkit to establish the best ways to ensure that the funding helps the poorest children.[9] This has been further embedded through Office for Standards in Education's (Ofsted's) guidance, which directs school leaders to the EEF toolkit. An evaluation of the Can Parent Pilot (Lindsey et al, 2014) showed that when a voucher was available, it was possible to stimulate the market for parenting classes and that parents who attended the classes reported an improvement in their sense of efficacy as a parent and mental well-being, as well as improvements in their child's behaviour. However, take-up of the classes was extremely low and the vouchers had no significant impact on the take-up. As discussed in Chapter Five, the best programme in the world will not change parenting behaviours if parents do not show up. Building supply without testing demand proved ineffective.

The Coalition government continued an activist family policy but the scope for state action was sharply reduced as families and children, alongside working-age adults, bore the brunt of austerity. The priorities shifted from a focus on child poverty to social mobility, and with it, an emphasis on building parents' and children's capabilities, while benefits cuts increased the pressures that families faced.

Family policy under the Conservatives

The results of the 2015 election were a surprise to all parties. There were strong indications from the polls during the campaign that no party would win an outright majority, and that some form of coalition government would continue, either Labour and Liberal Democrats, or Conservatives and Liberal Democrats. The Conservatives won with an outright majority, leaving much of the Liberal Democrat family policy ideas for the next term on the shelf. It also meant that the modifying influence on some Conservative policies was lost, and austerity would continue.

The ring fence on the Early Intervention Grant was finally removed in 2015, allowing local government to spend the funding allocation for early childhood services in any way they saw fit. The removal of the ring fence also made it increasingly difficult to find out how much local authorities were spending on family services, and how the spend was spread across targeted and open-access services. Between 2010 and 2017, spending on Sure Start children's centres fell by almost a half (Hayes, 2017).

The policy change that was the inspiration for the authors to write this book was the radical change in 2015 when the government removed income from its indicators of child poverty and abolished the statutory targets on child poverty and the duty on local authorities to have a strategy to reach those targets. The move was the culmination of a shift that had begun under the Coalition to redefine child poverty, inspired by the CSJ's *Breakdown Britain* report. The new Welfare Reform and Work Act 2016 included just two measurable indicators of children's life chances: growing up in a family without work and children's educational attainment at age 16. There were no indicators based on income or the early years. Attempts to remove the requirement to publish the four income-based measures of child poverty from the 2010 legislation were defeated in the House of Lords, but all targets on child poverty were removed, replaced with reducing worklessness and improving educational attainment. The Child Poverty and Social Mobility Commission was renamed the Social Mobility Commission. This was a watershed moment. In response to these changes to the child poverty legislation, Scotland used its devolved powers to reintroduce statutory targets on child poverty reduction in 2018.

Chancellor George Osborne's 2015 Budget made clear that austerity measures would continue, putting significant pressures not only on workless families, but also on children living in working households. Among the welfare cuts that had particular impact on families with children were:

- reducing the cap on overall benefits for a family from £26,000 to £23,000;

- further restrictions on large families were announced, with child tax credits only paid for the first two children; and
- the roll-out of UC, which has been slower, more difficult and, in many cases, punitive for claimants. Monthly payments have been particularly difficult for many benefit recipients, particularly when combined with sanctions, and delays in payments have left some families near destitution for weeks on end. (National Audit Office, 2018)

Further cuts to local authorities meant that funding available for family support services was reduced, along with increasing pressure on social care for elderly people. Many of the cuts were designed to be phased in over a number of years. The Office for Budget Responsibility responded to the 2015 Budget with predictions of increases in child poverty over the next ten years. The Institute for Fiscal Studies has predicted a seven percentage-point rise in relative poverty and a three percentage-point rise in absolute poverty by 2021/22 (Hood and Waters, 2017a). Consistent with the messaging of the Coalition, the Conservative government was particularly interested in reaching the *most disadvantaged*, so the Troubled Families initiative was expanded to more families.

David Cameron's period as Prime Minister of a Conservative rather than a Coalition government was short-lived. He resigned shortly after the European Union referendum result in June 2016. Nonetheless, a speech that he gave in January 2016 signalled his strong interest in social policy and his hopes for the future. In the speech, he promised a *social justice strategy*, a commitment not kept because of his departure from office. He rejected the Thatcherite approach that a growing economy will lift all boats, on the one hand, and Labour's approach that social policy can be solved through public spending, on the other. Some key elements of his concerns are reflected in the January speech:

In particular, too many are held back because of generational
unemployment, addiction or poor mental health....

some don't just get left behind; they start behind....

We need a more social approach ... one where we develop
a richer picture of how social problems combine, of how
they reinforce each other, how they can manifest themselves
throughout someone's life, and how the opportunity gap
gets generated as a result. (Cameron, 2016)

Cameron's solutions included: increasing the free childcare
entitlement to 30 hours per week for those in work in order
to make sure that employment income is not depleted by the
cost of childcare; investment in schemes to encourage savings;
and increasing funding for relationship support. However,
significant funding for relationship support failed to materialise.
While the speech also described the importance of the first
few years of life and of parenting support for new parents, the
specific offer was about speeding up adoption processes and
improving child protection services. Finally, he announced in
the speech the scaling up of Troubled Families. The Cameron
approach does not entirely leave out family income, but his
emphasis is still on the solutions to be found in changing
behaviour and targeting truly entrenched problems like long-
term unemployment, alcohol and drug problems, and anti-social
behaviour. He was very committed to improving the capabilities
of parents; however, at the same time other Conservative policies
substantially increased pressures on poorer families.

And then another Conservative prime minister: a different approach

Following Cameron's resignation, Theresa May became Prime
Minister in July 2016. Her speech on the steps of 10 Downing

Street was rich in promises on social policy. While her themes were continuations of the Coalition years, she expressed real commitment to social justice issues:

> That means fighting against the burning injustice that, if you're born poor, you will die on average 9 years earlier than others.
>
> If you're black, you're treated more harshly by the criminal justice system than if you're white.
>
> If you're a white, working-class boy, you're less likely than anybody else in Britain to go to university.
>
> If you're at a state school, you're less likely to reach the top professions than if you're educated privately. (May, 2016)

She also expressed concern for families who were *just about managing*: 'But the mission to make Britain a country that works for everyone means more than fighting these injustices. If you're from an ordinary working class family, life is much harder than many people in Westminster realise.'

Unfortunately, these lofty ambitions got lost in the immense task of managing the UK's departure from the European Union, alongside the commitment to continuing austerity. The Conservatives had a small majority and continued to be deeply divided on European issues. May had hoped to increase her majority by calling a snap election in June 2017. The surprise resurgence of the Labour Party under Jeremy Corbyn resulted in the Conservatives losing their overall majority, forcing May to rely on a confidence and supply agreement with the Democratic Unionist Party (DUP) from Northern Ireland.

May's hands were tied on family policy for several reasons. The DUP are socially very conservative and the Brexit negotiations are enormously consuming of government time and civil service resources. A possible additional constraint on May's willingness to comment on parenting is more personal. When running to be the Conservative leader, her opponent, Andrea Leadsom, commented on her unsuitability because she had no children. This was widely criticised in the press, and Leadsom withdrew the comment, but it may have left May's advisors wary of this territory. Such a comment also demonstrates how the political climate remains highly gendered; men's suitability for high office has never included questions of fatherhood.

In terms of an agenda about parents and poverty, May, like all her predecessors, saw employment as the best way out of poverty. She maintained the commitment to 30 hours of free childcare for families in work and the need to support vulnerable children and families but said little about wider family support issues. Families and children appeared on the final pages of the 2017 Conservative manifesto (Conservative Party, 2017). Overall, the approach to children and families has been fragmentary and piecemeal, with a number of initiatives. The most recent of these has been an important commitment to supporting the HLE as part of the government's social mobility strategy and renewed emphasis on the early years. A cross-government review of services for the under twos, including prenatal care, announced in July 2018, was being led by Andrea Leadsom, who chaired an earlier cross-party investigation on prenatal and infant care (Leadsom et al, 2014). This more recent review is likely to emphasise perinatal mental health for both baby and mother but is unlikely to consider poverty as a risk factor. The 2014 report made no mention of wider economic circumstances and their potential effect on mothers and babies.

In the brief period before May went to the country, there were two significant initiatives focused on children and young people led by then Secretary of State Justine Greening. The first was to put sex and relationship education on a statutory footing and gain a power to make Personal, Sexual and Health Education statutory in the future. This had long been a battle within Conservative ranks; her predecessor, Nicky Morgan, had attempted to bring it in but was overruled. It was a significant recognition of the need to give children and young people a broader education beyond academic subjects in order to equip them for life. Greening also introduced six 'Opportunity' areas across the country in social mobility 'cold spots' with a £60 million fund to support teaching and learning in those areas, more recently expanded to 12 areas by the next Secretary of State, Damian Hinds. However, Greening's reluctance to support the grammar school agenda resulted in her losing her job following the 2017 general election.

Support for relationships between parents has continued to receive attention with the publication of *Improving lives, helping workless families* (DWP, 2017b). The striking change from previous Conservative policies on the family is the shift in emphasis from the importance of marriage and stability to the quality of the relationship between parents, whether they are married, cohabiting, divorced or separated (see Chapter Three). The announcement came with an additional £30 million of funding for local innovation to grow services and interventions to support the inter-parental relationship and reduce conflict. This was to become the DWP's Relationship Conflict Programme, working in four regions of the country. However, the announcement coincided with the introduction of £12 billion of cuts in tax credits and benefits, prompting the accusation that the government was driving children and families into poverty and responding with a tiny pot of money to reduce family conflict, which was itself often the result of the stresses and strains of living on a very low income. Alongside this publication, the government produced a set of nine indicators to measure and monitor how workless families fare. There are two groups of indicators: parental disadvantages and children and young people's educational and employment outcomes. The document (DWP, 2017a) directly refers to the first group of indicators to meet the government's manifesto commitment to measure entrenched worklessness, family breakdown, problem debt and drug and alcohol dependency in an echo of the CSJ's *Breakdown Britain* report.

Early intervention is having something of a comeback. It is a key theme in the NHS ten-year plan and in two specific policy areas: children and young people's mental health, and knife crime. The first has been a response to the rising rate and salience of young people's mental health issues and the second has been a response to the rise in violent crime – in particular, knife crime. The Green Paper *Transforming children and young people's mental health provision* (Department of Health and Department for Education, 2017) makes the point that half of all mental health conditions are established before the age of 14 and that early intervention can play an important role. With a joint foreword by the Secretaries of State for Health and Education, it proposes a designated senior lead in every school and college, new mental health support teams, a four-week waiting time for specialist services and trailblazer areas. The Serious Violence Strategy launched in April 2018 stressed the need for a strategy that goes beyond law enforcement, including a range of different sectors and with an emphasis on prevention and early intervention. Propelled by the continued rise in serious violence and knife crime, the Home Office has created a £200 million Youth Endowment Fund to build the evidence for early intervention for 10–14 year olds who are at risk of youth violence.

In the early years, language development has become an issue of interest, related particularly to discussions about the HLE and the inability of some parents to provide the kind of rich language experience that paves the way for success in literacy and other outcomes later on. Theresa May was particularly vocal about gender equality, race equality and tackling domestic violence. Her commitment on race equality was backed up by the commissioning of the *Race disparity audit*,[10] which shows the extent of inequality affecting minority ethnic groups, particularly in employment. There have been two important announcements that indicate further liberalisation of the law in relation to couple relationships, a reflection of public policy catching up with changes in how families are leading their lives. The first is legislation to bring in no-fault divorce. This is particularly beneficial for children whose parents are caught in long-running conflictual cases. The second is a commitment to extend civil partnerships to heterosexual couples, supporting greater stability for parents and their children regardless of their sexuality and whether they choose to marry or form a civil partnership.

Over 2017–18, there has been increasing pressure to deal with the concerns about UC and the overall impact of benefit changes on poorer families. The view in some circles that there are no limits to how much money can be taken from poor families and not pay a political price has run its course. A combination of factors seems to be driving a rethink on UC: a very small parliamentary majority; pressure from across the political spectrum, as well as from citizen and voluntary sector organisations; and some softening of public attitudes to welfare spending. This was reflected in the 2018 Budget, which marked a change in the direction of government policy on public spending. Buoyed by an unexpected improvement in the public finances, alongside increasing public and political pressure from his own MPs, Chancellor Phillip Hammond announced an end to austerity. Analysis by the Institute for Fiscal Studies (Zaranko, 2018) addresses the question of whether austerity has ended or not. It shows that real departmental spending by 2023 is expected to be at similar levels to that of 2009–10, which, it could be argued, is an end to austerity. However, the picture varies depending on the area of spending; spending for unprotected departments is flat in real terms and falling once population growth is factored in. Austerity has not ended in relation to social security spending (Waters, 2018). While there has been an injection of cash into

UC (£1.7 billion) both to help with the transition and to reduce losses, £1.3 billion of the cuts to UC from the 2015 Budget remain (Resolution Foundation, 2018). Moreover, the other welfare changes – in particular, the two-child limit, the removal of the family premium and the benefits freeze – will result in substantial losses for those on low incomes, particularly those who are out of work. In response to strong lobbying from interest groups, the two-child limit policy has been modified to ensure that it will not impact on families with children born before April 2017, even if making a new claim. There is still a £4 billion cut to welfare benefits each year between now and 2023. The squeeze on families on low incomes continues, along with the pressure on local authority budgets to fund family support services. Moreover, the practical and political complexities of managing Brexit have absorbed massive time and civil servant resources, which could have been spent on the social justice issues that May wanted to address and are now left to her successor.

Labour's approach to families and children under Jeremy Corbyn

Labour's 2017 manifesto had a number of policies that aim to improve families' and children's opportunities, paid for through a substantial increase in taxation. Early years and childcare is promised as part of a National Education Service that goes from cradle to grave. There is continuity with the government's expansion of childcare but a commitment to shift to a system of directly subsidised provision, an increase in the number of graduate leaders in childcare settings and the protection of existing Sure Start centres. The manifesto calls for the United Nations Rights of the Child to be integrated into UK law and a new child poverty strategy that recognises in-work poverty. There are ambitious child health targets to reduce obesity, improve dental health and tackle mental ill-health. Labour's approach to welfare spending has been more ambivalent. The manifesto committed £2 billion to UC but did not commit to reversing the £7 billion of other welfare cuts, notably, the benefit freeze, benefit cap and two-child limit. However, following the 2018 Budget, Labour has committed to ending the benefits freeze.

Conclusion

As described in this chapter, successive governments have taken a keen interest in parents and parenting, shifting the role of the state in family life. Policies have intentionally reduced pressures and aimed to increase capabilities. More recently, policies have greatly increased pressures while simultaneously seeking to increase capabilities.

Labour policy concentrated on employment measures and income transfers to reduce child and pensioner poverty, while working-age adults without children were hardly thought of. The Coalition and Conservative governments brought in tax breaks that tended to benefit the top half of the income distribution for households with and without children and shifted the focus away from income poverty. Efforts to greatly reduce public spending have concentrated on benefits cuts for working-age adults and families, who have borne the brunt of the drive to reduce the deficit. Investment in mainstream services has also been substantially reduced, along with the increased targeting of many family services that were previously open access. The relatively small investments in relationship and parenting interventions are unlikely to prove successful against a backdrop of severe and increasing hardship. There can be no arguing that the rhetoric on fairness, opportunity and equality has not been matched by investment over the last ten years.

A combination of factors drove these changes in policy. Some were ideological, reflecting the political values of different administrations, notably, the scale of public spending and the size and role of the state. Other changes were driven by responses to external events: large events such as the global financial crash and its impact on the UK economy or the Brexit vote; as well as small but significant events such as Victoria Climbie's death despite being known to several public agencies. Policy changes were also driven by pressure from the public and civil society organisations, as well as new insights from research on how to solve long-standing issues.

However, despite the differences between the political administrations, there are also common features that run through the period. We see policies and legislation gradually catching up with changes in family structures, roles and norms; early years and childcare as a core part of provision; work–life policies built upon; a focus on building the capabilities of parents, couples and children; increased recognition of mental health and its impact; a focus on children and young people at risk; and the statutory minimum wage. Chapters Five and Six assess the success and failures of these policies, and offer considerations for the future of family policy.

Notes

1   See Cabinet Office (1999). See also: https://assets.publishing.service. gov.uk/government/uploads/system/uploads/attachment_data/file/260759/ 4181.pdf
2   See: www.tameside.gov.uk/yot/parentingorder
3   See: www.cypnow.co.uk/cyp/news/1031556/parenting-orders-a-little-help- for-parents
4   See: www.theguardian.com/commentisfree/2017/oct/10/behavioural- economics-richard-thaler-nudge-nobel-prize-winner
5   The fourth report was *The early years: Foundations for life, health and learning, an independent report on the early years foundation stage to Her Majesty's Government* by Dame Clare Tickell in 2011.
6   See: www.grahamallenmp.co.uk/static/pdf/early-intervention-7th.pdf
7   Other What Works Centres include the National Institute for Health and Clinical Excellence, the What Works for Children's Social Care and others (see: www.gov.uk/guidance/what-works-network#history).
8   See: http://policyinpractice.co.uk/under-the-hood-what-universal-credit- means-for-council-tax-support-schemes/

9   See: https://educationendowmentfoundation.org.uk/evidence-summaries/
    teaching-learning-toolkit/
10 See: https://assets.publishing.service.gov.uk/government/uploads/system/
    uploads/attachment_data/file/686071/Revised_RDA_report_March_2018.
    pdf

FIVE
IMPROVING THE LIVES OF CHILDREN AND FAMILIES

The vast array of policies, programmes, interventions and stated intentions described in Chapter Four is evidence of a growing acceptance across the political spectrum of a legitimate role for the state in family life. In this chapter, we assess how effective these policies have been in improving children's outcomes and life chances, especially for those who are in poverty or facing disadvantage. Policies over this period had differing goals: to reduce child poverty; to ameliorate the impact of poverty on a child's life chances; to improve social mobility; and, in some cases, to reduce inequality. We explore whether family policies were based on evidence or research, their effectiveness in improving both parent and child capabilities, and outcomes and whether they changed national patterns of opportunity and disadvantage over the 20-year period.

What role for evidence?

It is striking just how many of the policies discussed in the previous chapters drew on evidence and research from a range of different disciplines (for a discussion of different types of evidence and research, see Chapter Three). The use of data to identify, quantify and understand social problems has multiplied.

However, evidence of a need is not the same as evidence of what works to address the need. There has been a search for more effective solutions to address policy challenges, especially in the context of public spending pressures. The growing interest in Whitehall and elsewhere in evidence-informed public policy is illustrated by the creation and diversity of the What Works Centres and their earlier incarnations. They collectively represent a major investment by Labour, the Liberal Democrats and the Conservatives in the evaluation of social interventions. A particular and sometimes controversial feature of the What Works approach has been the application of scientific methods to *social* and *economic* issues, with a strong emphasis on the evaluation of public policy. Randomised Control Trials (RCTs) and Quasi-Experimental Designs (QEDs) have been increasingly used to determine whether an intervention has impact. While not all policies and practices can or should be subject to testing through RCTs, this approach enables us to estimate the direct causal impact of a policy on outcomes and may offer insights into how to improve it. However, there are risks in an overreliance on RCTs in evaluating social interventions (described in greater detail later in this chapter).

Of course, evidence is always evolving and did so over the last twenty years. Research findings and insights that had been buried in universities and academic journals, as well as new discoveries, made their way into political and policy consciousness over this period, for example, influencing the creation of Sure Start and the expansion in early years services under the Labour administration, the investment in parenting programmes that straddles Labour and the Coalition, and the more recent focus on relationship support under the Conservatives.

Evidence gathering does not happen in a vacuum, and nor does it determine policy. Political priorities and values shape the questions that are asked, as well as the solutions that are adopted. Politicians may ignore evidence if it is too challenging, impractical or does not fit with their own values or political viewpoint. At its best, an evidence-informed policy environment should enable experimentation and a rational light to be held up to current and future policy initiatives.

How effective were policies to support families and children?

We have seen that there is extensive research on the different factors that shape children's lives and future life chances. Bronfenbrenner's diagram in Chapter Three points to the need for policies to encompass societal, community, family and child-level factors. It is not possible to evaluate all the policies and interventions that we have discussed in this book. Instead, we explore the features and effectiveness of four approaches to improving children's outcomes:

- social security and tax credit policies that operate at a societal level to reduce poverty;
- early education and childcare to enable parents, especially mothers, to take up paid work, as well as improve school readiness for children;
- efforts to reform the system of support for families through service coordination and integration; and
- evidence-based programmes that work to a defined set of activities over a set number of sessions to improve parent–child interaction, the inter-parental relationship and children's cognitive and non-cognitive skills.

The first of these is clearly about reducing pressures on families; the second can both reduce pressures through increasing parents' incomes and, if high enough in quality, improve children's capabilities. Service integration may reduce pressures and/or improve capabilities. However, it is more about improving the way in which users access services and how those services respond. Evidence-based programmes are about increasing parents' and children's capabilities. Providing parents with techniques and skills for handling difficulties with children can also reduce pressures.

Social security benefits and tax credits

Reform of the social security and tax credit system is a primary and direct route to improving the living standards for children living in poor families. The Labour government's drive to end child poverty in a generation encompassed a wide range of policies directed at improving children's opportunities. However, the key drivers for boosting the incomes of families with children were increasing labour market participation, the National Minimum Wage, expanding childcare, reforming social security and the creation of tax credits. Here, we focus on cash benefits and tax credits.

Hills (2013) analyses the key features and impact of Labour's reforms to cash transfers on different groups of the population. Between 1996/97 and 2010/11, social security/tax credit spending in Great Britain rose from £114 billion to £181.5 billion, an increase of 61 per cent in real terms. Spending on family- and child-related benefits/tax credits accounted for nearly half of the real rise in spending, increasing from £16 billion to £40 billion. Over the same period, child poverty (60 per cent of median income after housing costs) fell by seven percentage points from 34 per cent to 27 per cent by 2010/11. There were reductions in poverty rates for children below the 40 per cent, 50 per cent and 60 per cent of median income thresholds, countering the criticism that the policy was designed to tip people just above the poverty line. The New Deal for Lone Parents, rising employment among lone and couple parents, and, to a limited extent, the National Minimum Wage[1] played some role in raising family incomes and thus reducing child poverty. However, the reduction was predominantly driven by the tax credits and benefit reforms (Joyce and Sibieta, 2013).

The analysis by Hills (2013) shows that the increases in tax credits and benefits going to families with children were effective in reducing child poverty over Labour's term of office. Nevertheless, there are a number of criticisms of the policy. First, tax credits going to families in paid work effectively subsidise employers to pay low wages. As a result, it is argued that these policies do not address the root causes of labour market inequalities. The National Minimum Wage does help to contain the subsidy by setting a floor beneath which wages cannot fall. However, job sustainability and upward mobility for low-paid and/or part-time workers was and remains a challenge, especially for mothers. Upward mobility in the job market for low-paid workers is the exception rather than the norm, particularly for women (Bastagli and Stewart, 2011), and measures to tackle this problem have had mixed success. More recently, there has a been a range of promising proposals that aim to address labour market inequalities by regulating the low-wage sector and increasing skills, training and progression paths for the low-paid workforce (Taylor, 2017; IPPR, 2018). However, these policies take time to embed and are unlikely to do away with the need for some cash top-up for families in low-paid employment.

Second, the commitment to reduce child poverty (and, indeed, pensioner poverty) came at the cost of an increase in poverty for those of working age without children. This is true, but when Labour came to power, it inherited one of the highest rates of child poverty in Europe, so there was strong justification to prioritise the next generation over and above other groups.

Third, a persistent criticism of the tax credit and childcare credit reforms was their impact on work incentives and their complexity. In relation to work incentives, Hills (2013) shows that incentives to go into work were broadly stable over the period, but there was a reduction in incentives to increase earnings for some of those already in work. Labour's tax credit reforms did, indeed, add layers onto an already complex system. Managing the system at the local level in order to ensure that families got what they were entitled to was extremely difficult. Adults move in and out of work, increase and decrease their working hours, have more children, get divorced, remarry, have serious health difficulties, and so on. All of these factors have to be taken into account in determining eligibility for a range of benefits, and family circumstances change over time.

The Conservatives have also been concerned about work incentives and the complexity of the social security system. Universal Credit (UC) is a major reform, designed both to increase incentives to go into work and to increase earnings for those already in work. It does so for one-earner couples but weakens the incentives for second earners, often women. UC assumes a family form – two parents with one earner – that is no longer the case for the majority of families with children. There are indications that the government is looking at the issue of women's circumstances again.[2] UC is also meant to address the problem of complexity but has been faced with similar challenges to Labour's tax credit policy of the fluidity of family life, along with severe cuts in the 2015 Budget. The 2018 Budget committed £1.7 billion of funding to help with the transition to UC; as a result, around three quarters of the funding that George Osborne took out of UC has now been put back (Resolution Foundation, 2018). A recent study from the Institute for Fiscal Studies (IFS) looks at the effects of UC on people's incomes over eight years. It finds that there are more losers than winners overall and that, on average, those in the lowest-income 10 per cent of the population lose the most from UC – a 1.9 per cent fall in their income, equivalent to £150 per year per adult. Of the 11 million adults entitled to UC once it rolls out, 1.6 million adults will gain by more than £1,000 per year but 1.9 million will lose at least that much.[3] However, for many, these losses are temporary. Three quarters of the losers fall into specific groups: those with financial assets greater than £6,000; the self-employed reporting low earnings; couples where one member is above state pension age; and some disability benefits claimants. Implementation problems persist and other benefit reductions continue to impact on the living standards of those on low incomes.

As described elsewhere, funding for services has also been severely cut, disproportionately affecting those most reliant on public services, low-income families. Some argue that the cost of Labour's measures was simply too high and distorted the balance of effort between income-based approaches and improving services. This argument ignores the huge increases in public services under Labour, including health, education and social care. New spending on children was split evenly between services and cash benefits (Stewart, 2013). The close attention to income measures was, in part, driven by the child poverty target embodied in one of the key Public Sector Agreements (PSAs) set by the Prime Minister's Delivery Unit.[4] While targets can have perverse effects, our view is that reducing income poverty is a critical element of a strategy to improve children's life chances. Reducing income poverty needs to be a twin-track approach: improving adults' access to better-paid jobs alongside income transfers. Income transfers are an efficient way to get resources not just to the child, but also to the wider family. The vast majority of parents use income for child-related spending (Gregg et al, 2006), so the money reaches its target group. We also know from the work cited earlier (Cooper and Stewart, 2017) that the effect size of spending on income-related measures is similar to those of education or early years. Income transfers are one of the few levers completely in the scope of central government. However, the sharp reduction in spending on social security in later years illustrates that this policy can readily be put into reverse.

Early years education and childcare

There is now a burgeoning body of work exploring the impact of early years education and childcare on children's outcomes.

Through rigorous evaluation, two influential American initiatives – Perry Pre-school High Scope programme for three and four year olds and the Abecedarian full day-care programme for children aged under five – showed the impact of high-quality pre-school education and care on both cognitive and social-emotional long-term developmental outcomes (Sylva et al, 2010). Both programmes were focused on children growing up in low-income high-risk families. Other studies reinforce these findings (Ruhm and Waldfogel, 2011). However, the impact of high-quality early years provision also benefits families from more advantaged homes, albeit to a lesser extent. Further research has unpacked the key features of good-quality education and care that have an impact on child outcomes: staff with good educational qualifications and training; sensitive and responsive styles of working; tailored learning; and high adult–child ratios (Waldfogel, 2006).

The case for investment in the early years was boosted by the US Nobel prize-winner James Heckman, whose econometric model demonstrated that the return on investment in children's services is correlated to the age at which the service was delivered. High-quality services in the early years were relatively inexpensive and yielded long-term gains. As children got older, interventions became more expensive and less effective. The 'Heckman Curve' became one of the most powerful arguments for the importance of targeting intensive family and child-focused services on poor children aged under five.[5] The programmes described earlier and other examples in the US were targeted at highly disadvantaged families; they were high in quality and had high participation rates. In many US studies, the cost savings are based on studies which show that a higher proportion of the control group compared to the intervention group wind up in prison, thus saving the state the costs of incarceration. As described later, replication of these programmes has proved challenging, not the least because most UK programmes, even if targeted, are aimed at a wider group of children. Fortunately, we do not have the levels of deprivation or the high levels of incarceration seen in the US.

In the UK, we also have evidence of the value of early education and care, albeit with a much wider population group than the US examples earlier. The evidence shows that when early years provision is high in quality, it can improve child outcomes well into teenage years (Hillman and Williams, 2015). A major longitudinal study of 3,000 children in pre-school provision (Evaluation of Pre-school, Primary and Secondary Education) showed sustained improvements in educational outcomes to GCSE level for those in high-quality pre-schools. The long-lasting impact was associated with the highest-quality settings. Disadvantaged children benefitted, especially when they attended a setting with children from a mix of backgrounds (Hillman and Williams, 2015). As Kathy Sylva et al (2010) puts it: 'the combination of a positive Home Learning Environment and a high quality pre-school setting put children on a very strong developmental pathway to success'. However, the evidence also shows that the quality is uneven, with better-quality provision in the maintained education sector than the private and voluntary sector. The vast majority of two and three year olds attend their free provision in the private or voluntary sector. Most four year olds are in school; only about a fifth of four year olds are in the private or voluntary sector (Department for Education, 2018). It is important to note that maintained education provision in the early years has been better funded and is more likely to have better-qualified and higher-paid staff. Unusually for social policy, children from less advantaged backgrounds are more likely to attend settings in the maintained sector; therefore, fortunately, the children likely to need the best-quality care are also more likely to get it (Gambaro et al, 2014; Gambaro and Stewart, 2015).

A more recent study by Jo Blandon and colleagues examined the impact of the expansion in the early 2000s of free early years education for three and four year olds. It found that while children who had accessed a free entitlement did better in assessments at the end of reception, the overall educational benefits are small and do not last (Blandon et al, 2018). It found evidence that poorer children benefited more from the free entitlement but that the effect was modest and did not narrow gaps in the long term. Unlike earlier research findings, the Blandon research was unable to find a difference between high-quality and low-quality nursery provision on child outcomes, using Office for Standards in Education (Ofsted) scores or staff qualifications as the measure of quality. However, they found substantial unexplained differences in outcomes between nurseries. It may be that Ofsted ratings and qualifications are failing to capture differences in practice between settings. These results are disappointing. It has been argued that there are methodological weaknesses in how children's outcomes are assessed in the study and the measures of quality used (Sylva et al, 2017).

As discussed in Chapter Four, it could also be argued that the main aim of the provision of early years services was childcare in order to improve female labour market entry rather than child development. However, the evidence on the impact of free childcare on mothers' labour market participation is mixed. Research by the IFS (Brewer et al, 2016) shows only limited impact of free childcare on mothers' employment and hours of work, though there were stronger effects for lone mothers and in the later time period when free entitlement to a part-time place became more generous and flexible. Data from Chapter Two show that over the last two decades, public attitudes to mothers taking paid work outside the home have changed dramatically. Employment of mothers is at an all-time high, reflecting, in part, the general increase in employment and the need for two incomes to maintain living standards. Provision for employment will prioritise affordability and flexibility; provision for child development will prioritise quality and consistency. These differences are typical of the maintained versus the private and voluntary sectors. The Blandon research looked almost exclusively at the private and voluntary sectors. This may illustrate that policymakers paid more attention to quantity than quality in the expansion of early years services; even our high quality may not be good enough, particularly if provision is mainly designed to ensure that mothers can work.

Service coordination and integration

Three major policy investments were among the many examples of the aim not only to increase provision of services for families, but also to improve the way in which local services worked together. Sure Start, Every Child Matters (ECM) and Troubled Families all emphasised both early intervention and interagency collaboration. However, they had significantly different features. Sure Start began as a programme aimed at all young children in particularly poor areas and grew into an open-access service throughout England. ECM, as described in Chapter Four, was a comprehensive redesign of the delivery of all children's services at the local authority level, including a common set of aims, common governance arrangements and the intention of information sharing across agencies. Troubled Families was highly targeted at the families with the most complex problems, but also aimed to use a variety of local agencies and services to *turn families around*. All three programmes were about ensuring that local children's and adults' services worked in a more coordinated joined-up way in order to ensure that families got a seamless set of services. Education, health, social care, the police, adult mental health services and housing all had a role to play.

Sure Start was meant to be the *glue* that joined services together and the *Polyfilla* that filled in the gaps between services for families with young children. Local areas were chosen based on child poverty data, and then local partnerships, including parents, were set up to decide what was needed to improve the life chances of under four year olds in the area. While early evidence from the National Evaluation of Sure Start (NESS) was disappointing (Belsky et al, 2007), results in the next two NESS studies were considerably better, particularly on results for mothers. The 2010 report compared children from the original NESS cohort group with similar children from the Millennium Cohort group. It found better health and lower body mass index for children, and mothers were found to have greater life satisfaction, an improved home learning environment (HLE), a less chaotic home environment and less harsh discipline (National Evaluation of Sure Start Team, 2010). Later studies, particularly the Evaluation of Children's Centres in England (ECCE) (Sammons et al, 2015), found positive results related to the frequency of use of centres, the numbers of named programmes on offer and interagency working. This major Labour flagship was beginning to show results after a disappointing start. Recent research (Catton et al, 2019) has examined the causal impact of Sure Start between 1999 and its high point in the 2000s on a number of health outcomes. It shows that Sure Start reduced the probability of hospitalisations among children aged 5–11 – equivalent to avoiding 5,500 hospitalisations of 11 year olds each year. Interestingly, the impact of Sure Start increases as children get older. The reduction in hospitalisations is driven by a reduction in infection-related entry to hospital for younger children and a reduction of accidents and injuries for older children. The authors also find that Sure Start benefits children in disadvantaged areas the most. They failed to find any evidence of impact on childhood obesity or maternal mental health. Publicly funded research generated huge amounts of evidence on what features delivered improvements in child and family functioning, and, as importantly, what was not working. Sadly, commitment to Sure Start progressively weakened during the Coalition years and has been under serious threat during the Conservative administrations. A recent study has shown dramatic cuts to funding for Sure Start children's centres, including closures, reductions in services on offer and reductions in opening times (Smith et al, 2018).

The dismantling of ECM began within 24 hours of the Coalition taking power in 2010. The Department for Children, Schools and Families went back to being a Department for Education and all ECM signage and references were removed. ECM is a good example of using years of research evidence about the nature of a problem to inform the design of solutions. ECM was driven by very high-profile investigations into child deaths. However, there is little evidence on the impact of the ECM reforms on child outcomes, in part, because such major structural change takes years to embed and even longer to show results. Evidence on other forms of integration of children's services indicate that while it is very difficult to establish a cause-and-effect relationship between child improvements and such reforms, there is good evidence on improvements in access to services and on data collection on children (Siraj-Blatchford and Siraj-Blatchford, 2009). Like Sure Start, the service reforms have been badly hit by austerity measures. ECM was hampered by the fact that schools were the only service that had no obligation to cooperate with other agencies. The translation of the ECM framework into a local context was sometimes overly bureaucratic. However, for the first time, there was a common framework for services to work together to improve child outcomes. The innovation of having a single senior official at the local authority level responsible for children has been eroded. These roles have largely been combined with other local authority functions to reduce management costs, resulting in a loss of focus and clarity on responsibility for child outcomes in the area.

Troubled Families is the only surviving example of service integration that spans Labour under the Family Intervention Projects (FIPs) banner, and then the Coalition and Conservatives as Troubled Families. Reinvigorated in 2011 under the Coalition because of riots, the decision to expand the programme in 2016 was criticised because the evaluation of the programme found little impact and poor value for money:

> The key finding from the impact evaluation using administrative data was that across a wide range of outcomes, covering the key objectives of the programme – employment, benefit receipt, school attendance, safeguarding and child welfare – we were unable to find consistent evidence that the troubled families programme had any significant or systematic impact.[6]

FIPs and Troubled Families were both based on a recognition that families with multiple risks were likely to experience persistent difficulties, which were also a substantial cost to the public purse. However, in its first phase, the Troubled Families programme was both light on evidence and failed to understand the dynamic nature of the issues and risks that families face. Local variation (driven by payments by results) in how the programme was delivered made it particularly difficult to evaluate. It may be that the programmes had statistically significant impacts in some areas that were outweighed by negative impacts in other areas (Bate and Bellis, 2018). There is also a question about the fit between the complex needs of some of the families in the programme and the support that was made available. This group of families is very likely to need intensive and persistent support provided by a range of appropriately qualified professionals, some working in adult services, others in children's services. Like Sure Start, early results of Troubled Families were disappointing, but the most recent evidence shows significant success in important areas: reductions in looked-after children; reductions in engagement with the criminal justice system; and improvements in employment (Ministry of Housing, Communities and Local Government, 2019).

Evidence-based programmes

Over a 20-year period, central and local governments have invested in a range of evidenced-based programmes to help support parenting, children and young people's development, and, more recently, the relationship between parents. All of these are core to prevention and early intervention, and their development has been part of a growing commitment to evaluate public policies in order to understand their effectiveness, impact and value for money. These programmes tend to be manualised and have a fixed curriculum and clear delivery structure, and some have been subject to rigorous evaluation. While evidence-based programmes have been a feature of public policy across the whole period, funding for them has been on a much smaller scale than the other initiatives we describe here.[7]

The Early Intervention Foundation assessed 75 programmes that aim to improve child outcomes through positive parent–child interaction in the early years. It looked at three outcomes: attachment, behavioural development and cognitive skills (Asmussen et al, 2016). It found that 17 programmes were well evidenced and a further 18 had preliminary evidence of impact on children. By 'evidence-based', we mean programmes that have had a robust RCT or QED that shows a positive impact on child outcomes.[8] Evidence was stronger for programmes that are targeted on risk, for example, a child's behavioural difficulties, delayed language development or lack of parental sensitivity, than universal programmes. There was also stronger evidence for programmes that focused on behavioural outcomes rather than attachment or cognitive development. This is likely to be because a greater number of programmes that focus on behaviour are targeted. The following case studies give examples of two evidenced-based early intervention programmes that have been implemented in the UK.

There is an international body of well-evidenced interventions to support the quality of the inter-parental relationship that has shown positive impacts on both couples and children; however, the UK evidence is still at an early stage. The Early Intervention Foundation identified eight programmes that had positive impacts, including reduced relationship conflict and disagreements, reduced depression and anxiety for parents, and improved child behaviours and mental health. They also showed positive impacts for children in poverty (Acquah et al, 2017). All of the interventions were developed internationally, but Incredible Years (IY) School Age Basic and advanced (see Case Study 2) has been widely tested and evaluated in the UK. Other programmes are being tested in four regions as part of the Department for Work and Pensions' (DWP's) Reducing Parental Conflict Programme for workless families.

Rigorous international evaluations have shown that some evidence-based programmes are effective, and some have been effectively replicated and adapted for the UK. For example, the ECCE study mentioned earlier has linked the use of such programmes to good outcomes in children's centres. However, replicating the impact of even the most promising programmes can be challenging. A considerable number of the programmes have been designed and tested in the US. The US has a much weaker social service infrastructure than the UK, and programme participants are often significantly more disadvantaged than UK families; hence, there is greater appreciation for any support on offer and greater scope for improvements from what is often a very low base.

Second, it is not straightforward to scale programmes for diverse populations and settings. Relatively few of the early intervention programmes have rigorous, long-term evaluation over different sites. Two case studies included here describe programmes that originate in the US and have an extensive international evidence base (see Boxes 5.1 and 5.2). Incredible Years (IY) – a parenting programme – has had a series of positive UK evaluations and has been widely implemented in the UK, especially in Wales. Family Nurse Partnership (FNP) has a long track record of success, but the latest UK trial showed no impact on the short-term primary outcomes of the programme, though did show some impact on children's cognitive development.

Third, the way in which a programme is implemented is critical. Implementing a programme successfully requires fidelity to the core ingredients of the programme while making some planned adaptations to the local context. This can be challenging for practitioners, who may feel deskilled by delivering a manualised programme. While middle managers may be convinced by the evidence of efficacy, local practitioners may feel that the introduction of such programmes is an implicit criticism of their usual way of working. It can also be challenging to reach the families that are most likely to benefit from a programme; families struggling with everyday life, a difficult child, little money, poor housing, conflict or substance abuse may find it hard to attend regular sessions. Participation requires practical support, including childcare, transport and appropriate venues. While families may seek help, they often do not go on to actually take it up or get lost in complex referral systems.

Relatedly, there can be a tension between the commissioning of evidence-based programmes that might be perceived as *top-down* and community-based approaches that may be popular and well received in a local context but either have not been evaluated or have been evaluated and found to have little or no impact. Moreover, high-quality evaluation is expensive. A bottom-up approach may be very promising but raising the funding to deliver such programmes is tough enough; achieving funding for evaluation is almost impossible. This does not mean that we should abandon evaluation; we need government, research councils and trusts/foundations to support good and proportionate evaluation if we are to learn what is or is not effective for whom under what circumstances.

The Sutton Trust and Esmee Fairbairn Foundation funded a project to address the problem of evaluation for smaller-scale voluntary sector-delivered parenting programmes. The project found that the most significant barrier to good evaluation was attracting enough participants of the intended audience to attend and stay the course (Barbour et al, 2018). Very small numbers of participants in any evaluation will limit the ability to establish effectiveness. Furthermore, on some open-access provision, parents who have less need may participate out of interest. While social mix can be beneficial, it can also lead to deadweight costs, expending resources on the *worried well* rather than those who could benefit the most.

Finally, many programmes are targeted based on particular risks. Early intervention is reliant on linking risks to the likelihood of poor outcomes in the future. Hence, the approach is predicated on key conditions: the ability to accurately identify risk; the availability of services to mitigate the risk; and the acceptability of the services to particular families while avoiding the stigma often associated with targeting. Targeting interventions precisely is important in terms of their likelihood of working – a child with significant behavioural difficulties will not benefit much from a light-touch universal programme. However, this requires effective training for those working in universal services such as GP surgeries and schools to be able to accurately identify risks.

As the evidence base of early intervention programmes develops, it should be possible to draw out the key features of successful interventions. These features could then form part of the initial training and ongoing professional development of the children's workforce. We also need to think about how such interventions fit within the wider system. The National Lottery Community Fund has financed A Better Start, a place-based initiative over ten years focusing on the early years (conception to three). A Better Start aims to improve three key areas of development: language, nutrition and attachment. It also aims to reform the wider system of children's services in the five areas where it is established. Evidenced-based innovations are more likely to have wider impact when they become integrated into the normal way of working. However, the infrastructure for the implementation and scaling up of evidence-based interventions is sorely lacking. While there is funding for innovation, little is in place to ensure that a minimum offer for families is available and accessible everywhere. This exacerbates inequalities given the differential ability of families to weather shocks and the differential support needs of different families, as well as the same families over time.

BOX 5.1 FAMILY NURSE PARTNERSHIPS

FNP is a programme where a specially trained nurse practitioner works intensely with pregnant teenage mothers through home visits from pre-birth until the child is aged two. Initially introduced under the Labour government in 2007, it expanded substantially under the Coalition government with the creation of an independent National Unit in 2012, reaching a large number of local authorities.

Developed in the US, it is based on a 40-year international evidence base with a strong track record of improving children's mental health and well-being, preventing child maltreatment, and enhancing school achievement and employment, among other outcomes, in both the US and Holland. The most recent evidence from Building Blocks, an RCT undertaken in the UK in 2015, found that the programme had had no impact on the primary outcomes: birth weight, breastfeeding, smoking and the space between subsequent births. It did find a modest impact on child cognitive skills and language outcomes at age two. However, following this evaluation, the FNP National Unit has been testing out new approaches to make FNP more flexible, personalised and cost-effective.

Source: Drawn from the Early Intervention Foundation guidebook (available at: https://guidebook.eif.org.uk/) and the 'FNP adapt interim report' (FNP and Dartington Service Design Lab, 2018)

BOX 5.2 INCREDIBLE YEARS

The IY Preschool Basic programme is for parents with concerns about the behaviour of a child between the ages of three and six. Parents attend 18 to 20 weekly group sessions where they learn strategies for interacting positively with their child and discouraging unwanted behaviour. Two facilitators (Qualifications and Credit Framework level 7 or 8)) lead parents in weekly two-hour group discussions of mediated video vignettes, problem-solving exercises and structured practice activities addressing parents' personal goals. The Advanced add-on to IY Preschool includes a component that seeks to improve children's outcomes by improving the quality of inter-parental relationships.

IY was initially developed in the US and has a strong international evidence base developed over 30 years. IY Preschool has evidence from three RCTs, all of which were conducted in the UK. The trials found improved child outcomes, an increase in positive parenting and a reduction in negative parenting and parental symptoms of depression and stress. IY has been widely implemented in the UK, in particular, in Wales and Northern Ireland.

Source: Drawn from the Early Intervention Foundation guidebook (available at: https://guidebook.eif.org.uk/)

In all four approaches to supporting children and families, we see successful features alongside implementation challenges. We now turn to look at the bigger picture in order to understand the impact of policies and the wider context on children's outcomes over the period.

How have policies changed national patterns of advantage and disadvantage for families and children?

Having reviewed a number of approaches and interventions, we now look more broadly at how children and families have fared over the last two decades. Data, of course, lag behind reality; changes in policy and the wider environment take time to translate into outcomes for children and families. Some policies will have an impact long after they are implemented, both positive and negative.

We begin by looking at what happened to public spending on children and families over the last two decades. This is not because we equate spending itself with good outcomes necessarily, but because public spending patterns provide a lens through which to understand the way in which public policy priorities have shifted over time.

Public spending on children

Over the last two decades, the scale and patterns of public spending have changed substantially. Some of those changes reflect wider economic and demographic shifts, such as employment rates and the child population; others reflect changes in public policy. Here, we look at what happened to spending on children over the period, exploring different areas of spending: benefits, early years education and children's services. We draw extensively on a comprehensive analysis undertaken by the IFS (Kelly et al, 2018) commissioned by the Children's Commissioner for England. This analysis shows that in 2017/18, total spending (excluding health care) on children was over £120 billion, over £10,000 per child under 18. This is 42 per cent higher in real terms than it was in 2000/01, but 10 per cent lower than the high point in 2010/11.

Looking more closely at public spending on *benefits*, the IFS compared spending per child and per pensioner. In Table 5.1 we see a 61 per cent increase in spending per child in the first ten-year period and a fall of 17 per cent in the second ten-year period. Pensioners show a very different pattern, with a 29 per cent rise in the first ten-year period and a fall of just 1 per cent in the second ten-year period.

Not surprisingly, these changes in spending on benefits have translated into changes in the incomes of families and children. Browne and Philips (2010) show increases in the net

Table 5.1: Summary of *benefit* spending per head for children and pensioners

	Spending per child	Spending per pensioner
Level in 2000/01 (2017/18 prices)	£3,570	£7,967
Percentage change 2000/01 to 2009/10	61%	29%
Percentage change 2009/10 to 2019/20	−17%	−1%
Percentage change 2000/01 to 2019/20	33%	27%
Level in 2017/18 (2017/18 prices)	£4,995	£10,345
Level in 2019/20 (2017/18 prices)	£4,733	£10,147

Source: Kelly et al (2018: 17, Table 3.2)

incomes of workless families of between 12 per cent and 16 per cent under the Labour government, with smaller rises for pensioners. Browne and Elming (2015) show that low-income families experienced a fall in income of around 6–7 per cent as a direct result of tax and benefit reforms under the Coalition government. IFS analysis (Hood and Waters, 2017b) shows the anticipated impact of changes since 2015, assuming the full implementation of UC, which indicates a fall of over 15 per cent in net household income for the poorest 10 per cent of working-age households with children, compared with under 2 per cent for pensioners.

Looking at the same period, patterns in spending on *early education* are rather different and reflect the fact that early years services have become an enduring part of the education system and welfare state. Table 5.2 shows spending per child for different parts of the education sector. We see the most rapid rises in overall spending on early education (from a very low base) in the first ten

Table 5.2: Summary of *education* spending per pupil levels and changes over time

Phase of education	Spend per pupil, 2000/01 (2017/18 prices)	2000/01 to 2009/10 (% real-terms change)	2009/10 to 2019/20 (% real-terms change)	2000/01 to 2019/20 (% real-terms change)	Forecast spend per pupil, 2017/18 (2017/18 prices)	Forecast spend per pupil, 2019/20 (2017/18 prices)
Early years	£1,307	+58%	+17%	+85%	£2,056	£2,415
Primary schools	£2,990	+49%	+8%	+61%	£4,810	£4,810
Secondary schools	£3,881	+50%	+7%	+61%	£6,239	£6,239
Further education (16–18)	£4,439	+27%	–5%	+21%	£5,567	£5,354

Source: Kelly et al (2018: 28, Table 4.2)

years as the early years entitlement was extended to more children and for more hours per week and more weeks in the year.

Early years spending per child (Kelly et al, 2018) rose by 58 per cent between 2000/01 and 2009/10, and is expected to rise by a further 17 per cent by 2019/20 as a result of the increase in childcare to 30 hours per week for parents in work. However, providers of early years services have said that the additional funding to support the extra free hours is not sufficient, and some private nurseries have gone out of business. Insufficient funding is a particular risk to quality. Better-qualified staff are known to deliver higher quality services, but they are more expensive. Further education has fared less well than early years through both periods. Spending for 16–18 years olds had lower rises in spending per young person over the first ten years (27 per cent) than other areas of education and has fallen in real terms by 5 per cent in the subsequent ten years. This reflects what we would argue is a gap in policy thinking on late adolescence (see Chapter Six).

Children's services spending doubled from £4.8 billion in 2000/01 to £9.7 billion in 2009/10 (Kelly et al, 2018). This includes Sure Start, which grew from £500 million to £1.7 billion over this period. Since then, spending on children's services fell by 11 per cent until 2017/18, and if the trend continues, it would be a reduction of 14 per cent by 2019/20. Once the rise in the number of children since 2009/10 is taken into account, the fall in spending per child is likely to be about 20 per cent in real terms over the second ten years. Critically, the composition of children's services spending has changed substantially between 2009/10 and 2016/17, with a much greater focus on looked-after children – a 22 per cent real-terms rise while spending on safeguarding and family support was unchanged. Meanwhile, over the same period, spending on Sure Start fell from £1.7 billion in 2009/10 to 0.7 billion (a 41 per cent fall) and young people's services from £1.4 billion to £0.5 billion (a 64 per cent fall).

These marked rises and then falls in overall spending on children's services and the refocusing of the remaining funding on children in care is a consequence of both the substantial and long-running rise in the number of children being taken into care and the 49 per cent real-terms reduction of funding to local authorities since 2010. The majority of the cuts in local services for vulnerable families have occurred in the most deprived 20 per cent of councils (Kelly, 2018).

In 1997, there were 30,000 children in care in England, compared with just over 72,000 in care in 2017.[9] Taken at face value, one might assume that these figures indicate a massive increase in child maltreatment and neglect. However, the measurement of increases or decreases in abuse is highly problematic. Records are often inaccurate or incomplete, and how abuse is defined has changed over the years. Policy and practice on removing children from parental care are constantly in flux and often responsive to high-profile cases of abuse and/ or child deaths. While social workers may feel pressure to reduce high risk by lowering the care threshold, the pressure on budgets may push in the opposite direction. The Care Crisis Commission concluded that the rises in looked-after children reflected a combination of factors, including an increase in poverty and deprivation, changes in policy and practice, and reductions in the availability of early help and prevention services (Family Rights Group, 2018). The dramatic reductions in spending on Sure Start and preventive services documented earlier have meant that local authority budgets are increasingly focused on statutory responsibilities alone. Furthermore, entry barriers to services are raised, meaning that some families who would have been eligible for specialist help are deemed not sufficiently needy. In our view, this is a major issue for the life chances of children. Services designed to provide lighter-touch support when problems are not serious and entrenched are virtually non-existent in many areas. Interventions provided early enough to prevent serious deterioration are no longer available. Efforts to increase capabilities are offered too late as pressures on families increase.

These changes in the pattern of public spending on families and children represent important shifts in the how the welfare state has supported families over the last two decades. We see not just a rise and then fall in public spending on children and families before and after 2010, but some striking shifts in the pattern of spending driven by changing economic circumstances, political priorities and public attitudes. There was a huge rise in financial support for families and children through tax credits and social security changes from 1997 to 2010. Then followed a big decline, though spending still remains high. After 2010, pensioners were protected and individual taxpayers benefited from the very generous increase in the personal income tax threshold – a tax cut that is blind to children. Preventive spending in local authorities has fallen since 2010, with Sure Start children's centres, youth services and early intervention – all focused on the more disadvantaged – severely hit. At the same time, we have seen investment in universal childcare grow both before and after 2010, the 'pro-poor' focus of funding on schools growing, and the NHS relatively protected compared to other services (Kelly, 2018).

Alongside these seismic shifts in the landscape of public spending and tax cuts, there have been changes in the public perception and legitimacy of different approaches to supporting families. Universal services – schools and the NHS – still command widespread support and this now extends to childcare, where the changes in women's working patterns make it a political priority across political divides. While attitudes to welfare benefits have softened (see Chapter Two), spending on welfare is still a much lower priority than other areas of the welfare state. Spending on programmes to support parenting and couple relationships is tiny compared to the big-ticket items discussed here, but there is arguably a greater acceptance for the state to fund services that support family relationships, bolstered by the rise in mental health difficulties among children and young people.

Poverty and inequality

In Chapter Four, we described how the last two years of the Labour government and then how the Coalition and Conservative governments responded to the financial crash of 2008. In short, Labour under Gordon Brown attempted to protect poorer groups by continuing with social expenditure. Public spending as a proportion of gross domestic product (GDP) increased, along with a rising deficit and debt. The Coalition and the Conservatives developed a range of social policies but debt reduction was a primary policy aim that required sharp cuts in public spending, reducing both income transfers and services for families.

What happened to child poverty over our 20-year period? The Resolution Foundation's *Living standards audit* (Corlett et al, 2018) analysed child poverty rates over time. It looked at the original Households Below Average Income (HBAI) survey data and then adjusted these data to account for a substantial under-reporting of benefit receipts in the survey. It also includes what the Resolution Foundation calls a 'now-cast' to predict future patterns. Figure 5.1 shows the trends over time using 60 per cent of median income after housing costs as the poverty threshold; it compares the original HBAI data with the *adjusted measure*. Both show similar patterns, with child poverty decreasing between 1998/99 and 2004/05, rising in the run-up to the financial crash, falling again from 2007 to 2010/11 and rising thereafter, with a sharp rise anticipated after 2016/17. The adjusted measure shows a sharper fall in child poverty over the first period and a sharper rise in the later period. On this measure, the Labour administration hit its first target of reducing child poverty by a quarter by 2004 and was close to hitting its second target of halving child poverty by 2010. One

Figure 5.1: Child poverty reductions in the 2000s may have been faster than previously thought

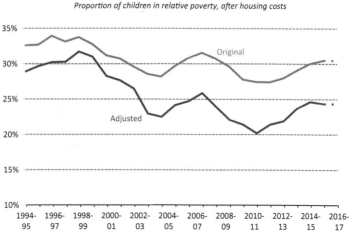

Proportion of children in relative poverty, after housing costs

Source: Corlett et al (2018: 67, Figure 43)

of the difficulties of using the HBAI child poverty measure (60 per cent of median household income) is that it shows poverty falling through the recession, which was partly because median incomes were falling but also because Gordon Brown boosted measures to protect families with children. The Social Metrics Commission (2018), an independent and non-partisan body, has established a new measure of poverty that is also a relative measure but takes into account a wider range of resources and costs, and smoothes income over time. It does not cover data before 2001, but after that date, it shows similar trends in how poverty rates changed over time, with one important exception – it shows higher rates of poverty during and after the financial crisis. A welcome development is the DWP's announcement that it will publish poverty statistics based on the Social Metrics Commission measure on an experimental basis; this could help to encourage future governments to do more to tackle income poverty.[10]

The changes in child poverty over time reflect both the wider economic circumstances and the policies of different governments. The focus on eradicating child poverty under Labour, with the substantial resources invested in benefits, tax credits and, to a lesser extent, active labour market programmes, led to a significant fall in the number of children in poverty. The impact of reductions in welfare payments as part of austerity policies and the proposed roll-out of UC are reflected in the sharp rise in child poverty that is predicted by 2020.

Income inequality is linked to levels of relative poverty. John Hills et al (2019) looked at patterns of income inequality and poverty over the last 50 years in the UK and found that years with lower income inequality tend to have lower relative poverty and vice versa. This is not the result of how poverty or inequality is measured. The research shows that the relationship between income inequality and relative poverty is not constant, and that policies or other factors can make a difference. Trends in overall inequality over the last 20 years show that inequality was broadly stable after the marked rise in inequality that occurred in the 1980s. However, child poverty was declining through active policy in the first decade. The Resolution Foundation looks at three different measures of inequality over time, making the same adjustment to account for the under-reporting of benefit receipts. The adjustment leads to a somewhat lower level of inequality over the period for all three measures. However, the gap between the top and the bottom remains very high by post-war standards, reflecting global trends in inequalities.

Social mobility for families and children

While we have concentrated on the lens of poverty to assess interventions and policies through most of this book, it is important to look at outcomes across the income distribution and socio-economic groups. As we noted earlier, there is a gradient in children's outcomes and families move in and out of poverty and low income, so policy cannot simply focus on the poorest families. Moreover, it also matters what higher-income groups are doing and how they are faring; it is very difficult to close the gap if the bar is ratcheted ever upwards. Here, we ask to what extent does a child's future success depend on the family into which they are born? Are life chances determined when life has barely started?

Our kids, the American dream in crisis, by Robert Putnam (2015), explored the growing gap between the experiences of children in affluent and poor homes – features such as parental time, extra-curricular activities and parental engagement that impinge on later opportunities. In 2016, the Social Mobility Commission undertook a similar analysis to explore how far the UK echoed this pattern (Richards et al, 2016). The report provides a rich source of data on socio-economic status and indicators of family life under three domains that have been shown to be particularly important for children's life chances and social mobility. The three domains are: parent engagement, children's behaviour and parents' social networks. It found that the picture in the UK was more positive than the US, but that there remain substantial challenges. There are socio-economic gaps between families under each of these domains, with particularly sharp inequalities in relation to cultural activities and parents' social capital and some aspects of communication. The Social Mobility Commission report found that there were improvements and a narrowing of inequalities over time for a number of outcomes (see Figure 5.2): truancy, helping with homework, attendance at parents' evenings at school and the frequency with which mothers read to their children. Consistent with the research noted in Chapter Two, time spent with children and fathers reading to children showed improvements for most children but greater improvement for better-off children, hence a widening of inequalities. For issues such as conduct problems, emotional symptoms, hyperactivity and civic engagement, there was an increase in class inequalities (no data were available for whether

Figure 5.2: Changes in social mobility over time by outcome

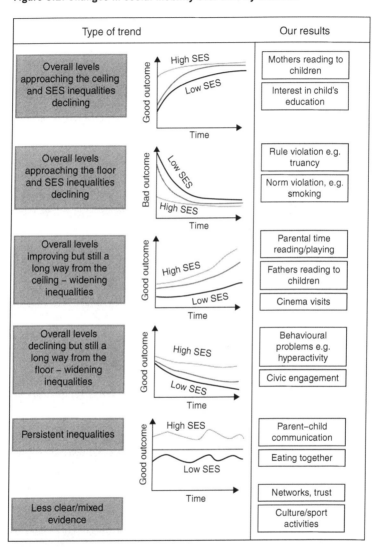

Source: Richards et al (2016)

the incidence is increasing or not). The authors stress the importance of not focusing on schooling as the sole response to improving social mobility, but instead drawing on a wider range of drivers.

There are some worrying signs of increases in the gaps between poorer children and their more affluent peers. The Social Mobility Commission's (2019) *State of the nation* report finds that social mobility has been 'virtually stagnant' since 2014. Infant mortality rates, which had been falling for the lowest income groups since 2007, appear to have been on the rise over the last two years,[11] though it is still too early to detect a firm trend. Mental health difficulties are on the rise. The most recent analysis[12] shows that depressive symptoms have risen over the last ten years – levels of depression have increased by 9 per cent for young people born in the early 1990s to nearly 15 per cent for those born in 2000/01; self-harm has increased as well. Gender differences persisted, with girls more likely to be depressed and self-harming, but rates of increase were similar for both girls and boys. Children who were born in 2000/01 were more likely to sleep less during the week, to be obese and to have poorer body image in comparison with those born in the early 1990s. More positively, anti-social behaviour and substance use had declined over this period.

Conclusion

We have looked at how children and families have fared over a period of 20 years and we see a mixed picture. Changes in the overall pattern of advantage and disadvantage are the result of both wider socio-economic/demographic factors and policy changes. The marked fall in unemployment since its high point in 2011 to its lowest level in 43 years is a positive development but has not been reflected in similar falls in levels of poverty. This is because having a job is not a guarantee of escape from poverty – until very recently, wages have flatlined and the labour market has become more precarious. There has been a substantial reduction in overall spending from 2010, reflecting the impact of the financial crisis and a shift in government policy response to the recession. Within that spending envelope, spending on social security/tax credits for children and families declined sharply over the second decade and is leading to an increase in child poverty now and in the future. Alongside this change has been a sharp fall in local authority spending, which has had a particular impact on the funding of early intervention, parenting support and Sure Start children's centres. The second decade also saw an increasing emphasis on families with deep and complex disadvantages. Other areas of policy show greater continuity, with the commitment to gender equality, work–life balance and childcare and early education maintained and expanded.

We see that there is good evidence for the impact of policies to address income poverty and the role of high-quality early education on children's overall development and longer-term outcomes. There is also good evidence for a number of evidenced-based programmes to support the parent–child relationship and other early intervention programmes, but there remain key challenges in relation to their funding and replicability. The Troubled Families programme has helped improve the relationship between key workers and families with complex needs, and recent evidence has shown impact on some child outcomes. Service reform has been tried with some success in relation to joining up services, but major reforms such as ECM have been short-lived. The Social Mobility Commission's report shows that there have been important areas of progress over the last two decades in parental interest and active engagement with children's education, as well as a fall in adolescent smoking, alcohol and drug taking, but behavioural problems are on the increase and persistent inequalities remain in some areas such as parent–child communication.

We also face new challenges for family policy – Brexit will bring economic uncertainty, at least in the short term, and a declining influence of the European approach to social policy and social rights (Stewart et al, 2019). There is a growth in the geographical divide between larger cities and their hinterlands, as well as between the North and the South-east of England. Rapid technological change is leading to major challenges, not only relating to future jobs and skills, but also shaping our everyday lives, including how we consume, communicate and live in localities. There are new risks for families and children, with growing rates of mental health difficulties, rises in suicides for young people (especially for young men), sharp rises in childhood obesity and, in some areas, an explosion of knife crime among teenagers leading to horrific injuries and deaths. We continue to struggle with ensuring real equality of opportunity and outcomes for black and minority ethnic children, as well as children with disabilities.

The overall conclusion from this chapter is that income transfers and services can improve the life chances of children and young people. It is possible to flatten the social class gradient in a range of child outcomes by providing services that reduce pressures and increase capabilities. However, there is no magic bullet. Identifying which services are most effective for whom is complex. Deciding on the balance of investment in generous benefits with the provision of effective services is even harder. In Chapter Six, we explore what this might mean for family policy in the future.

Notes

[1] The National Minimum Wage had only a modest impact on reducing child poverty because many low-paid individuals are not living in low-income households.

[2] In a speech on 11 January 2019, Amber Rudd, Secretary of State for Work and Pensions, indicated that she will consider changes to UC to take account of women's circumstances.

3 See: www.ifs.org.uk/publications/14085

4 PSAs were introduced under the Labour government as an accountability mechanism to help measure and drive the delivery of key manifesto promises and flagship policies.

5 See: https://heckmanequation.org/resource/the-heckman-curve/

6 See: www.theguardian.com/society/2016/oct/17/governments-448m-troubled-families-scheme-has-had-little-impact-thinktank

7 There is no overall estimate of the funding of evidence-based programmes as most have been locally commissioned.

8 See: https://guidebook.eif.org.uk/eif-evidence-standards

9 See: https://assets.publishing.service.gov.uk/government/uploads/system/uploads/attachment_data/file/664995/SFR50_2017-Children_looked_after_in_England.pdf

10 See: www.gov.uk/government/news/new-poverty-statistics-developed-to-help-government-target-support

11 See: www.theguardian.com/society/2019/apr/19/newborn-baby-deaths-may-be-on-rise-among-poorest-in-england

12 See: https://cls.ucl.ac.uk/depression-is-on-the-rise-among-young-people-but-antisocial-behaviour-is-down-new-research-shows/

SIX
LEARNING FOR THE FUTURE

In this final chapter, we briefly review what we have learned and then look at some tensions that are inherent in family policy, poverty reduction and the role of the state. The chapter also discusses two cross-cutting themes: the misuse of science; and policy and research gaps. Finally, we propose some building blocks that should inform approaches in the future.

What have we learned?

The evidence presented in Chapter Three gives us a clear idea about what matters most for children to thrive when looking at their cognitive, social and emotional development:

- Money matters in its own right, not only in terms of the ability to buy goods and services that promote healthy development, but also because the lack of money is a key factor in parental stress.
- Parents also matter. A good home learning environment can make a real difference to children's learning and attainment as well as their social and emotional development. However, it is harder to provide such an environment for children when income is low.
- Parents' – especially mothers' – educational background and their mental health are particularly important for how children

fare. Different aspects of family resources matter for different outcomes: income, education and social class are all important. Persistent poverty and hardship are particularly damaging.

• Relationships matter, not only between mothers, fathers and their children, but also between mothers and fathers. Good relationships between parents in intact or separated families are a protective factor for children.

We have explored the changes in the direction of family policy between governments, driven by political perspectives, external events, public attitudes and civil society. We know that policy and interventions can make a difference, and there are a number of strategic lessons for policy that we draw from the last two decades.

If we are to make a lasting impact on children's life chances, government policy needs to encompass macro- and micro-factors. The year 2010 marked the end of a dual approach to improving children's outcomes through the reduction of child poverty *and* increasing parents' and children's capabilities. Under the Labour administration, the commitment to reduce child poverty ensured that policy measures and investment were focused on this crucial driver of children's life chances. Targets are not without problems – they can lead public policy to prioritise the short over the long term. However, the child poverty target ensured that an issue that does not command the public support that universal services such as schools or the National Health Service (NHS) do was high up the political agenda. The shift in policy direction since 2010, with major cuts in benefits and tax credits and the abolition of the child poverty income targets, has meant that those of working age and families with children have borne the brunt of austerity measures, particularly those on low incomes. As a result, child poverty is on the rise and predicted to get significantly worse.

The story of Sure Start – from a flagship policy with the ambition of a centre in every neighbourhood to a struggling service today – provides some important lessons. It was a bold new service, providing parent-centred, integrated, inter-professional and evidenced-informed services. However, it takes time to embed a new service, especially a cross-cutting one that requires different services to work together and share data. While the case for Sure Start was firmly rooted in the evidence, practice within centres was variable. Evaluations were initially mixed; however, they gradually improved, with the latest evaluation showing that, in its heyday, Sure Start was making a substantive difference to children's health. With hindsight, the political ambition to expand the service from deprived areas nationwide was premature and led to resources and focus being diluted. This is testament to just how long it takes for new initiatives to embed; they require not only sustained investment, but also time to implement and learn from mistakes.

In contrast to policy on poverty and Sure Start, there has been much more continuity across political administrations when it comes to early years and childcare provision. The early years and childcare is now a core and virtually universal service. The Pupil Premium introduced under the Coalition government helped to focus funding on more disadvantaged children. However, investment to improve the quality of childcare provision has lagged far behind the drive to increase the volume of places. We know about many of the key features of quality: the importance of graduate leaders, improving the skills and wages of the early years workforce, child–teacher ratios, and pedagogical practice. There is much more to do here when it comes to investment and implementation. This matters for all children, but particularly for the disadvantaged.

The boundaries of family policy have shifted. There has been an increasing recognition in public policy of the importance of relationships *within* families in shaping children's and adults' life chances and well-being. In the past, this was seen as belonging largely to the private sphere, being the responsibility of families themselves unless there were major difficulties (for example, divorce, domestic violence or abuse and neglect). Labour's policies were primarily focused on the child and parents, sidestepping questions of marriage and family stability, although there was some investment in relationship support. Under the Conservatives, there has been a strong emphasis on family stability and marriage, though this has increasingly shifted to a focus on the *quality* of relationships between parents, whether married, cohabiting, divorced or separated. This is a positive development that grasps the need to support the wide diversity of families and their journeys.

Prevention and early intervention have been features of public policy across the period, albeit with limited public investment. In practice, governments at the central and local level have found it very difficult to shift the focus from reactive and acute services to preventive and early support services. This is particularly the case at a time of austerity, when many of the early intervention services have fallen under the axe. Social investment has had only a limited impact through funding particular programmes, rather than enabling systemic change.

There has been a commitment across all the political administrations to work with high-risk families. The importance of working with the whole family and their wider networks is well established. However, the lessons from the Troubled Families programme is that working with families with complex needs requires sustained engagement and professional support.

Tensions to be managed

There are a number of inherent tensions and challenges in devising effective family policies. First, politicians' time spans are short; they want to show progress within a Parliament but making lasting improvements in children's capabilities and life chances takes time. There is little institutional memory within the civil service, so sustaining a policy across different political administrations is difficult. We underestimate the difficulties of implementation, the need to test, learn and adapt.

Second, public policy necessarily involves trade-offs, navigating between competing priorities, interests and finite resources. It needs to consider whether state action is likely to be successful in solving the issues identified. If it is, at what level should it engage: national, regional, local or neighbourhood? Should it be a regulator, funder or provider? Evidence on whether interventions are value for money is a useful tool to help with making trade-offs. While this is growing, especially in the What Works Centres, it is still fairly limited when it comes to assessing wider policies and services.

Third, there are limits to top-down policymaking. While public policy has a critical role to play in supporting children's outcomes, it is broader than the state. Not everything is best done through the state; it can be disempowering and also fail. Some state-mandated services are designed to avoid bad things from happening, like the regulation of safeguarding procedures, but they may be so specified that they also stifle innovation. There is a recurring tension between a bottom-up approach to developing a new initiative, where community engagement substantially shapes a policy or service, and one that is driven by evidence of impact that is tightly specified and commissioned by central or local government or public agencies. Co-production is when the community and local residents work alongside public bodies to redesign services that should be more responsive to local needs and more likely to have local buy-in. The challenge for co-production is that, inevitably, not all those for whom the service could be useful are involved in the design. Those most in need may be the least likely to participate. Indeed, their participation may be discouraged by other members of the local community. The evidence on community-led initiatives is still in its early stages. However, it is clear that without local service-user engagement, an intervention cannot succeed. If the intended group do not want to use the service, it will not work. However, just because they use it and enjoy it, and say it made a difference, it may not be shown to have made a long-lasting impact on child outcomes.

Fourth, family policies have attempted to cater for *all* children, *poor* children and children growing up in families with *multiple difficulties*, but the balance between these has shifted over time. Under Labour, policy spanned universal, open-access and targeted services. Under both the Coalition and Conservative periods, the emphasis shifted, with a growing focus on policies targeted at high-risk families, with the exception of childcare and the early years. Inevitably, there is a tension between universal and targeted services. Universal services are high in cost because everyone can access them, but they sometimes miss those most in need, who may require strong encouragement to make use of services. Targeted services often miss those just below the threshold, who could benefit from light-touch support that may prevent difficulties getting worse. Furthermore, the narrative on families in poverty over the years has increasingly morphed into a narrative on families with complex problems, defining poverty in relation to particular family disadvantages that are not specifically about money. While most families with complex problems also tend to live on a low income, the majority of low-income families do not have several complex problems. Their biggest problem is not having enough money. The solution to a lack of income rests with more income and/or lower costs of essential expenditure. Along with more generous social security benefits, we need better-paid employment and controlling or subsidising the costs of housing, childcare and other necessities.

Evidence misused or missing: infant brain development

While the emerging science of infant brain biology is exciting, it has been used in a UK context that is problematic in two ways: it presents a deterministic view that all is lost if early experiences are less than optimal; and it is discussed in the absence of consideration of the wider systemic issues that affect child outcomes, particularly poverty and poor housing. Ever since the path-breaking publication of *From neurons to neighborhoods* (Shonkoff and Phillips, 2000), there has been a growing interest in infant neurobiology. The report brought together all that was known about brain science, as well as what services could have the most impact. Its title is telling – it ranges from neurons to neighbourhoods – the full spectrum is important. It provides evidence for the importance of the early years without the more recent associated view that without appropriate caregiving for infants and toddlers, the cause is lost:

> Early experiences clearly affect the development of the brain. Yet the recent focus on 'zero to three' as a critical or particularly sensitive period is highly problematic, not because this isn't an important period for the developing brain, but simply because the disproportionate attention to the period from birth to three begins too late and ends too soon. (Shonkoff and Philips, 2000)

In the UK, the translation of what we now know about optimal experiences for infants that encourage normal brain development has been turned into a narrative which implies that all is lost if infants are not appropriately nurtured. The language describing brain science includes words like *architecture of the brain and foundations*, implying a bricks-and-mortar metaphor of permanence in structure and function. As discussed in Chapter Three, we know that while the early years is a time of particular sensitivity, brain development continues well into adulthood. Not only is the science misunderstood, but in policy terms, it leads to assumptions that risk exposure in early years is irretrievably damaging. How can we hope to maximise every phase of development if it is assumed that there is no hope for some children past the age of five?

An additional risk in the UK narrative on brain development is that the social context of poverty and poor environments is absent, concentrating mainly on parental experiences and behaviours. In the UK, the interest in pregnancy and the first two years was set out in *Building great Britons, the first 1001 days*, a report produced for the All Party Parliamentary Group for Conception to Age 2 (2015). This report makes no reference to the wider issues of family poverty, poor neighbourhoods and pressures on families. Its main thrust is about the critical phases of brain development and attachment, and what is presented as irretrievable damage if early development is put at risk by poor parenting and dangerous parenting behaviours: 'Just as a positive environment can support optimal development for babies, so too can a negative environment disrupt development, with potentially lifelong damaging effects on the developing brain which can predispose to mental health problems, risk-taking behaviour, depression, anxiety and even violence throughout the lifespan' (All Party Parliamentary Group for Conception to Age 2, 2015). While no mention is made of poverty, the behaviours described as most dangerous to pregnant women and young babies are implicitly class-biased. The narrative implies that if only all pregnant women, their partners and new parents conformed to certain good behaviours and refrained from other bad behaviours, all young children would grow up to be productive taxpaying citizens. Government's role is to help with the capabilities of parenting, while no role is acknowledged in reducing the pressures of low income, poor housing or poor neighbourhoods. Parenting, especially if experienced for the first time, can be truly daunting in the first few months. Over the last ten years, advice for parents has been strongly associated with interpretations of neuroscience that leaves middle-class parents fearful of doing the wrong thing, and low-income parents subject to unfair judgements about their parenting skills by the professionals who contact them. The language of *toxic stress*, irretrievable damage caused by alcohol and drug misuse, domestic violence, and harsh home environments is strongly associated with families in poverty. At the same time, well-off families believe that baby Mozart and flashcards for infants will enable their children to succeed in an increasingly competitive environment for places at better schools and better universities. Sadly, in neither case are we allowing ourselves and our offspring the luxury of enjoying childhood for its own sake as opposed to an investment for some ideal future.

Absence of policy and research

Finally, important research and policy gaps remain. There has been less attention paid to the adolescent period and how parents can support teenagers and young people making the transition to adulthood. Government policy segments child development into distinct age phases: under-fives, school-aged children and post-16. However, family policy, including parenting, crosses departmental boundaries – education, employment, housing and health – each with a slightly different emphasis, and sometimes with conflicting policy goals. Such structures cannot be avoided; work has to be distributed in some way, but the structure often determines what gets left behind. Not surprisingly, school-aged children are dealt with mainly within education policy. No government can be accused of failing to address education; it has been of strong interest for at least the last four prime ministers. Children are often referred to as pupils, determining their status by the institution. Education policy has chiefly been concerned with school structures, pedagogy and workforce. It has been less concerned with parents and the wider social issues that impact on child attainment, health and well-being. So, parent support and family policy has focused much less on post-primary-aged children.

For parents, the teen years can be particularly challenging. Respecting the emerging needs of young people for agency while continuing to protect and provide for them is a delicate balance. Unlike very young children, where problems tend to centre on bedtime routines, eating and potty training, the errors of young adults can have much more profound impacts: teen pregnancy, alcohol and drug misuse, and peer relationships for good or ill. Neighbourhood plays a much stronger role as home influence reduces. Parents are more likely to be in full-time work and so have less time to meet for support. Moreover, there are no obvious venues for casual mutual support for the parents of teens. They no longer wait at the school gate, attend, stay and play at the children's centre, or attend library sessions. The parenting of teenagers is altogether lonelier, and sharing difficulties is potentially more stigmatising.

Unlike the early years, *late* adolescence lacks an academic narrative that helps shape policy. Research funding is often driven by policy interest; for this group, both policy and research are relatively thin. An exception is Hagell's (2012) *Changing adolescence*, which brings together a series of articles and data on how adolescent lives are changing and Schoon (2018) on *Supporting Youth Transitions*. Under Labour and the Coalition, the main emphasis on the later school years was about attainment and widening access to university. As we saw in Chapter Five, public spending per pupil in the further education sector has fallen in real terms over the last decade, after rising in the first decade, and is now lower than spending per pupil in schools. For Labour, the goal in England was for 50 per cent of all young people to go to university, and for all young people to achieve five A–C grades at GCSE level. While these goals drove significant improvements in school performance, they carried significant risks, especially for young people in the bottom half of the income distribution. As described in Chapter Four, the Labour government did invest significantly in this age group through the Education Maintenance Allowance (EMA), Connexions service and the targeted work on reducing teen pregnancy. The teen pregnancy work achieved remarkable success and EMA increased educational participation, but Connexions had little evaluation of efficacy and was dismantled by the Coalition government. Under the Coalition and Conservative governments, the emphasis shifted; with the exception of the Citizens Service, the focus has been on families with multiple difficulties through the Troubled Families programme and those with highly aberrant behaviours: teen gangs, the radicalisation of young Muslims and the trafficking of young girls. More recently, there has been a major initiative on children's and young people's mental health and a new emphasis on technical and vocational skills, with a review of tertiary education due to complete at the time of writing.

Think tanks including the Sutton Trust and the Resolution Foundation have become increasingly interested in the disadvantages experienced by young people, particularly those not heading for the top-class universities. In 2010, David Willetts's (2010) influential book *The pinch – How baby-boomers took their children's future, and why they should give it back* was published. It has taken several years for its messages to influence public policy proposals. The Social Mobility Commission (2017) has also reported on the growing gap in life chances for the generation of young people born between 1980 and 2000 – the Millennials. This group has suffered from stagnating wages, high housing costs, reliance on a largely insecure private rented sector and significantly fewer opportunities for progression in work compared to their forebears. Young people in their 20s and early 30s are much more likely to be living with their parents than 20 years ago. Parenting is going on for much longer. The parents of this group of young people become *the bank of mum and dad*, yet again underlining intergenerational disadvantage for those young people whose parents cannot afford to support them into early adulthood.[1] This recent interest in young adults is welcome, and it is long overdue. However, the story is still fragmented. There is no coherent policy framework that brings together support for adolescents and their parents that encompasses their education and training, physical and mental health, and relationship support.

So, where do we go to next? We cannot simply turn the clock back; policy has to be fit for current and future challenges.

Building blocks for the future

Virtually all parents want the best for their children. However, as a society, how can we cast our gaze wider, beyond our own families, to foster a sense of shared responsibility for the next generation, a shared commitment to support children's well-being and future capabilities? What would it take to create a child-friendly society? How do we create the conditions for parents, children and young people to be able to chart their own futures?

Government at the central and local level has a legitimate role to play in both reducing pressures and increasing capabilities for families. Pressures can be reduced by a fair welfare state with adequate benefits reflecting real living costs. The state has a critical role to play in addressing child poverty, both through tackling the labour market drivers of low earnings for parents, and through the redistribution of incomes. Income matters, but so does access to affordable, quality housing, transport and childcare. Government plays a key role in financing, regulating and/or providing these services. The safety net of basic provision needs urgent repair if families are not to find themselves destitute. Publicly funded services and specific interventions also play a key role in supporting the mental health of mothers and fathers, parenting skills, and the inter-parental relationship – all of which are central to children's well-being and longer-term cognitive, social and emotional development.

Policies in the areas of redistribution through progressive taxation, housing and employment are big systemic changes that require government intervention. Policies designed to increase parental capabilities are significantly less expensive but are challenging to implement and replicate. We are still learning about the most effective approaches. This is an area where we need to continually test and learn. Moreover, both sets of policies arouse strong public attitudes for and against. Convincing the public that both are important is a major task for any politician seeking election.

Services can reduce pressures as well as increase capabilities. A public health approach to services encompasses universal, open-access, targeted and highly tailored support. It enables primary prevention and early intervention. A universal platform of entitlements is essential because all families and individuals across income groups have needs at particular times in their lives. A universal offer is also the most efficient way to identify some people who have additional needs of a short- or longer-term nature. Once offered, universal services are very difficult to withdraw; they attract widespread public support. Open-access services are often provided by voluntary organisations. They are not part of entitlements, nor are they targeted. Local areas make decisions on the appropriate level, type and locality of open-access family support services. Unfortunately, such services are likely to be the first to go as funding is stretched, but they play a vital role in reaching out to those just below entry barriers for targeting and often encourage the development of community cohesion among diverse groups. Services also need to reflect the dynamic nature of family life, flexing to meet needs at key transitions from conception to young adulthood, and to adapt to a much more diverse set of family structures and circumstances.

New technologies are increasingly becoming part of the service mix, creating accessible forms of communication between practitioners and parents/children, direct access to information, and group-based forums to share knowledge and experiences between users. The trick is to ensure that innovations are enabling for families and children and narrow rather than widen the gap. The ubiquity of smartphones has been a great leveller in access to new technologies. While smartphones and computers have created new ways of learning and playing, they have also brought risks: children are more sedentary, less likely to play outside and subject to cyber-bullying and increased social anxiety through social media. Screen time has been linked to the disruption of sleep patterns and many other risks. Policies are slowly catching up with new technologies, but we are a long way from exploiting new technologies in ways that enhance the lives and opportunities of low-income families and children.

Government, in partnership with employers, has played a major role in creating a much more family-friendly employment environment. Work–life balance is a critical factor in enabling parents to have more time with their children to engage with, play with, support and guide them. However, more could be done. Maternity pay is significantly below the National Living Wage, making it almost impossible for women on very low wages to take their full leave entitlement. Fathers are still much less likely to take time off to look after their children. This is, in part, a reflection of the gender pay gap, but it is also a reflection of the disparity in entitlements for fathers and mothers, as well as cultural expectations about men's and women's roles – though this is changing. A Scandinavian-style *daddy leave* (take it or lose it), as well as higher rates and longer periods of paternity pay, could help to shift the balance.

Creating a child- and family-friendly society also rests on fostering an intergenerational bond to share responsibility for the next generation. Grandparents play a vital role in relation to childcare and kinship care for children where there are safeguarding concerns. There have been a range of community initiatives that bring the different generations together – from older people going into classrooms to help with reading and play, to bumps and babies groups taking place in old people's homes. These encounters benefit both the older and the younger generations, and there is great potential to think about how to design intergenerational contact into the lived environment and provision of public, private and community services.

Finally, all new and existing policies need regular evaluation and review. For whom do they work and under what circumstances? Is the policy intention clear and focused? Is there agreement about the problem that the policy is trying to solve? Are there clear measures to know if the solution is working? Most importantly, do the people for whom the policy or intervention is intended agree that there is a problem to solve and have a role to play in the design of the solutions? Enhancing the voice of children, young people and parents in identifying the issues that matter to them is a critical component of effective policymaking and responsive services.

In summary, what would an ideal system look like? Key features might include:

- key entitlements that set out what every child, family and individual can expect from the state – health care, childcare, education, adequate housing, transport, parenting and relationship support, and a minimum income;
- a public health approach that encompasses prevention, early intervention and tailored responses to families at high risk;
- flexibility in the system that responds to the dynamic nature of family life over the life course and the varying needs of different communities and family types; and
- transparent and regular data collection to identify where and for whom systems are working and where they are failing to catalyse effective responses.

There is no doubt that all political parties now consider the family a legitimate domain for policy and delivery. All politicians seek elected office to make changes and improve the lives of residents. However, all parties have a long way to go to ensure that reducing child poverty as well as growing the capabilities of parents and children is the lens through which all policies are assessed. Future public policy needs to put both these goals on an equal footing. It will take significant investment to restore and improve benefit levels. We also need to invest in the provision of traditional community services: children's centres, youth clubs, libraries and children's play areas. Where will the co-production of innovations happen if there is no place for local parents to meet?

It will take many years of substantial investment to strengthen the shaky infrastructure on which new technological and community solutions will be developed, tested and spread. To achieve the goals mentioned earlier, big decisions need to be made not only about money, but also about the role of local government vis-a-vis Westminster, the role of government in redistribution across income groups and the current unfairness between the generations. Learning from the past is not an attempt to recreate it; it is an attempt to avoid the mistakes that were made and adjust our sights for the future.

Note

[1]   See: www.resolutionfoundation.org/advanced/a-new-generational-contract

References

Acquah, D., Sellars, R., Stock, L. and Harold, G. (2017) *Interparental conflict and outcomes for children in the contexts of poverty and economic pressure*, London: Early Intervention Foundation.

All Party Parliamentary Group for Conception to Age 2 (2015) *Building great Britons conception to age 2, the first 1001 days*, London: Wave Trust and PIPUK.

Asmussen, K. (2011) *The evidence-based parenting practitioner's handbook*, Abingdon: Routledge.

Asmussen, K., Feinstein, L., Jack, M. and Chowdry, H. (2016) *Foundations for life, what works to support parent–child interaction in the early years*, London: Early Intervention Foundation.

Asmussen, K., Law, J., Charlton, J., Acquah, D., Brims, L., Pote, I. and McBride, T. (2018) *Key competencies in early cognitive development: Things, people, numbers and words*, London: Early Intervention Foundation.

Axford, N. and Berry, V. (2018) 'Perfect bedfellows: why early intervention can play a critical role in protecting children', *British Journal of Social Work*, 48: 254–73.

Barbour, L., Eisenstadt, N., Goodall, J., Jelley, F. and Sylva, K. (2018) *Parental engagement fund*, London: Sutton Trust.

Bastagli, F. and Stewart, K. (2011) *Pathways and penalties: Mothers' employment trajectories and wage growth in the Families and Children Study*, CASE/157, London: Centre for Analysis of Social Exclusion, London School of Economics.

Bate, A. and Bellis, A. (2018) *The Troubled Families programme (England)*, Briefing Paper, Number CBP, 07585, 18 July, London: House of Commons Library.

Bellis, M.A., Lowey, H., Leckenby, N., Hughes, K. and Harrison, D. (2014) 'Adverse childhood experiences: retrospective study to determine their impact on adult health behaviours and health outcomes in a UK population', *Journal of Public Health*, 36(1): 81–91.

Bellis, M.A., Ashtoni, K., Hughesii, K., Fordii, K., Bishopi, J. and Paranjothy, S. (2015) *Welsh Adverse Childhood Experiences (ACEs) study, adverse childhood experiences and their impact on health-harming behaviours in the Welsh adult population*, Wales: Public Health Wales, NHS Trust.

Belsky, J. (2001) 'Developmental risks (still) associated with early child care', *Journal of Child Psychology and Psychiatry*, 42(7): 845–59.

Belsky, J., Barnes, J. and Melhuish, E. (2007) *The National Evaluation of Sure Start, does area-based intervention work?*, Bristol: Policy Press.

Blakemore, S.J. (2018) *Inventing ourselves: The secret life of the teenage brain*, London: Transworld Publishers.

Blandon J., Hansen, K. and McNall, S. (2018) *Evaluating the impact of nursery attendance on children's outcomes final report*, IoE, University of Surrey, London: Nuffield Foundation.

Brewer, M., Cattan, S., Crawford, C. and Rabe, B. (2016) *Free childcare and parents' labour supply: Is more better?*, IFS working paper, London: Institute for Fiscal Studies.

Bronfenbrenner, U. (1989) 'Ecological system's theory', in R. Vasta (ed) *Annals of child development*, 6, Greenwich: JAI Press.

Browne, J. and Elming, W. (2015) 'The effect of the Coalition's tax and benefit changes on household incomes and work incentives', Institute for Fiscal Studies (IFS), Briefing Note BN159. Available at: www.ifs.org.uk/publications/7534

Browne, J. and Phillips, D. (2010) 'Tax and benefit reforms under Labour', Institute for Fiscal Studies (IFS), 2010 Election Briefing Note No. 1. Available at: www.ifs.org.uk/bns/bn88.pdf

Burchardt, T., Obolenskaya, P., Vizard, P. and Battaglini M. (2018) 'Experience of multiple disadvantage among Roma, Gypsy and Traveller children in England and Wales', Centre for the Analysis of Social Exclusion, LSE, Case Paper 208.

Bywaters, P., Kwhali, J., Brady, G., Sparks, T. and Bos, E. (2017) 'Out of sight, out of mind: ethnic inequalities in child protection and out-of home care intervention rates', *British Journal of Social Work*, 47: 1884–902.

Cabinet Office (1999) 'Guide to the centre of government part III: the modernizing agenda'. Available at http://www.cabinet-office.gov.uk/moderngov/whtpaper/index.htm

Cabinet Office (2017) *Race disparity audit summary findings from the ethnicity facts and figures website*, London: Cabinet Office.

Cameron, D. (2007) 'Civility and social progress', speech to the Royal Society of the Arts, 23 April.

Cameron, D. (2016) 'Life chances for all', 11 January.

Cancian, M., Mi-Youn, Y. and Shook Slack, K. (2013) 'The effect of additional child support income on the risk of child maltreatment', *Social Service Review*, 87(3): 417–37.

Cattan, S., Conti, G., Farquharson, C. and Ginja, R. (2019) *The health effects of Sure Start*. Available at: www.ifs.org.uk/publications 14139 London: Institute for Fiscal Studies.

Chartered Institute of Housing and Resolution Foundation (2014) *More than a roof: How incentives can improve standards in the private rented sector*, London: Chartered Institute of Housing and Resolution Foundation.

Children's Commissioner for England (2018) *Vulnerability report 2018*, London: Office of the Children's Commissioner.

Chote, R., Crawford, R., Emmerson, C. and Tetlow, G. (2010) *Filling the hole: How do the three main UK parties plan to repair the public finances?*, 2010 Election Briefing Note No. 12 (IFS BN99), London: Institute for Fiscal Studies, Nuffield Foundation.

Cmd 6404 (1942) Social Insurance and Allied Services; Report by Sir William Beveridge, London: HMSO.

Cobb-Clark, D., Salamanca, N. and Zhu, A. (2016) *Parenting style as an investment in human development*, Working Paper 2016, Bonn: Institute for the Study of Labour.

Commission on Social Justice and IPPR (Institute for Public Policy Research) (1994) *Social justice, strategies for national renewal*, London: Vintage.

Conservative Party (1997) *You can only be sure with the Conservatives*, London: Conservative Party.

Conservative Party (2010) *Invitation to join the government of Britain, the Conservative manifesto 2010*, Uckfield, Sussex: Pureprint Group.

Conservative Party (2017) *Forward together, our plan for a stronger Britain and prosperous future*, London: St Ives PLC.

Cooper, K. (2016) *CASE, Centre for the Analysis of Social Exclusion, annual report 2016*, CASEreport 112, London: LSE.

Cooper, K. (2017) 'Poverty and parenting in the UK', PhD thesis, London School of Economics and Political Science (LSE).

Cooper, K. and Stewart, K. (2013) *Does money affect children's outcomes? A systematic review*, York: Joseph Rowntree Foundation.

Cooper, K. and Stewart, K. (2017) *Does money affect children's outcomes? An update*, CASE paper 203, London: LSE, Centre for the Analysis of Social Exclusion.

Cortlett, A. and Judge, L. (2017) *Home affront: Housing across the generations*, London: Resolution Foundation.

Corlett, A., Clarke, S., D'Arcy, C. and Wood, J. (2018) *The living standards audit 2018*, London: Resolution Foundation.

Crawford, C., Goodman, A. and Greaves, E. (2013) *Cohabitation, marriage, relationship stability and child outcomes: Final report*, IFS Report 87, London: Institute for Fiscal Studies.

CYPN (Children and Young People Now), Children's Society and NCB (National Children's Bureau) (2015) *Cuts that cost, trends in funding for early intervention services*, London: NCB.

DCSF (Department for Children Schools and Families) (2010) *Support for all: The families and relationships Green Paper*, London: HMSO.

Del Bono, E., Francesconi, M., Kelly, Y. and Sacker, A. (2016) 'Early maternal time investment and early child outcomes', *Economic Journal*, 126(596): 96–135.

Department of Health and Department for Education (2017) *Transforming children and young people's mental health provision – a Green Paper*, Cm 9523.

Dermott, E. (2008) *Intimate fatherhood: A sociological analysis*, London and New York, NY: Routledge, Taylor & Francis Group.

De Vaus, D., Gray, M., Qu, L. and Stanton, D. (2015) *The economic effects of divorce in six OECD countries*, Research Report No. 31, Canberra: Australia Institute of Family Studies.

DfE (Department for Education) (2018) *Provision for children under five in England*, London: HMSO.

DfES (Department for Education and Skills) (2003) *Every child matters*, Norwich: The Stationery Office.

DfES (2007) *Every parent matters*, Nottingham: HMSO.

Dotti Sani, G.M. and Treas, J. (2016) 'Educational gradients in parents' child-care time across countries, 1965–2012', *Journal of Marriage and Family*, 78(4): 1083–96.

DWP (Department for Work and Pensions) (2017a) *Improving lives: Helping workless families, analysis and research pack*, London: HMSO.

DWP (2017b) *Improving lives, helping workless families*, London: HMSO.

DWP (2019) *Households below average income (HBAI) summary tables*, London: National Statistics.

Early Intervention Foundation (2018) *Realising the potential of early intervention*, London: Early Intervention Foundation.

Economic Dependency Working Group (2009) *Dynamic benefits*, London: Centre for Social Justice and Oliver Wyman.

Eisenstadt, N. (2011) *Providing a sure start, how government discovered early childhood*, Bristol: Policy Press.

Family Rights Group (2018) *Care crisis review: Options for change*, London: Nuffield Foundation.

Faux, T. and Platt, L. (2015) *Parenting and contact before and after separation*, London and Canterbury: LSE and University of Kent.

Feinstein, L. (2003) 'Inequality in the early cognitive development of British children in the 1970 cohort', *Economica*, 70(277): 73–98.

Feinstein, L. (2015a) 'Social class differences in early cognitive development: a response from Leon Feinstein', *Longitudinal and Life Course Studies*, 6(4): 476–83.

Feinstein, L. (2015b) 'Social class differences in early cognitive development and regression to the mean', *Longitudinal and Life Course Studies*, 6(3): 331–76.

Feinstein, L. (ed) (2015c) *Social and Emotional Learning, Skills for Life, Overview Report*, London: Early Intervention Foundation.

Field, F. (2010) *The foundation years: Preventing poor children becoming poor adults*, London: Cabinet Office.

Fitzsimons, E. and Villadsen, A. (2018), *Father departure from the household and childhood mental health: how does timing matter*, London: Centre for Longitudinal Studies Working paper 2018/1, Institute for Education/UCL.

FNP (Family Nurse Partnership) and Dartington Service Design Lab (2018) 'FNP adapt interim report'. Available at: https://fnp.nhs.uk/media/1246/fnp-adapt-interim-report.pdf

Gambaro, L. and Stewart, K. (2015) 'A question of quality: do children from disadvantaged backgrounds receive lower quality early childhood education and care?', *British Education Research Journal*, 41(4): 553–74.

Gambaro, L., Stewart, K. and Waldfogel, J. (2014) 'Equal access to early childhood education and care? The case for the UK', in L. Gambaro, K. Stewart and J. Waldfogel (eds) *An equal start? Providing quality early education and care for disadvantaged children*, Bristol: Policy Press.

Goldstein, H. and French, R. (2015) 'Differential educational progress and measurement error', *Longitudinal and Life Course Studies*, 6(3): 331–76.

Goodman, A., Sibieta, L. and Washbrook, E. (2009) *Inequalities in educational outcomes among children aged 3 to 16*, report for the National Equality Panel, London: IFS.

Goodman, A., Joshi, H., Nasim, B. and Tyler, C. (2015) *Social and emotional skills in childhood and their long-term effects on adult life, a review for the Early Intervention Foundation*, London: Early Intervention Foundation, Cabinet Office and Social Mobility Commission.

Gopnik, A. (2016) *The gardener and the carpenter: What the new science of child development tells us about the relationship between parents and children*, London: Vintage.

Gordon, H., Acquah, D., Chowdry, H., Sellers, R. and Feinstein, L. (2016) *What works to enhance interparental relationships and improve outcomes for children?*, London: Early Intervention Foundation.

Gregg, P. and Wadsworth, J. (eds) (1999) *The state of working Britain*, Manchester: Manchester University Press.

Gregg, P., Waldfogel, J. and Washbrook, E. (2006) 'Family expenditures post-welfare reform in the UK: are low income families with children starting to catch up?', *Labour Economics*, 13(6): 721–46.

Hagell, A. (ed) (2012) *Changing adolescence, social trends and mental health*, Bristol: Policy Press.

Harold, G., Acquah, D., Chowdry, H., Sellers, R. and Feinstein, L. (2016) *What works to enhance interparental relationships and improve outcomes for children?*, London: Early Intervention Foundation.

Haux, T., Platt, L. and Rosenberg, R. (2015) 'Parenting and post separation contact', CASE paper 189.

Hayes, D. (2017) 'Labour highlights 40% cut in children's centre spending', *Children and Young People Now*, 11 December.

Heath, P. (2009) *Parent–child relations: Context, research and application* (2nd edn), New Jersey, NJ: Pearson.

Hick, R. and Lanau, A. (2017) *In work poverty in the UK: Problem, policy analysis, platform for action*, London: Nuffield Foundation and Cardiff University.

Hick, R. and Lanau, A. (2019) 'Tax credits and in-work poverty in the UK: an analysis of income packages and anti-poverty performance', *Social Policy and Society*, 18(2): 219–36.

Hillman, J. and Williams, T. (2015) *Early years education and childcare: Lessons from evidence and future priorities*, London: Nuffield Foundation.

Hills, J. (2013) *Labour's record on cash transfers, poverty, inequality and the lifecycle 1997–2010*, CASE/175 Centre for Analysis of Social Exclusion, London: London School of Economics.

Hills, J. (2017) *Good times bad times, the welfare myth of them and us*, Bristol: Policy Press.

Hills, J., McKnight, A., Bucelli, I., Karagiannaki, E., Vizard, P., Yang, L., Duque, M. and Rucci, M. (2019) *Understanding the relationship between poverty and inequality, overview report*, London and York: Centre for Analysis of Social Exclusion and Joseph Rowntree Foundation.

HMG (Her Majesty's Government) (2010) *Child Poverty Act 2010 Chapter 9*, London: HMSO.

HMT (Her Majesty's Treasury) (2004) *Choice for parents, the best start for children: A ten year strategy for childcare*, Norwich: HMSO.

HMT (2009) *Budget 2009: Building Britain's future, economic and fiscal strategy report and financial statement and budget report*, London: The Stationery Office.

HMT (2011) *The magenta book, guidance for evaluation*, London: Crown Copyright.

HMT and DfES (Department for Education and Skills) (2007) *Policy review of children and young people, a discussion paper*, Norwich: HMSO.

Home Office (1998) *Supporting families*, London: HMSO.

Hood, A. and Waters, T. (2017a) *Living standards, poverty and inequality in the UK: 2016–17 to 2021–22*, London: Institute for Fiscal Studies.

Hood, A. and Waters, T. (2017b) 'The impact of tax and benefit reforms on household incomes', Briefing Note BN196, Institute for Fiscal Studies (IFS). Available at: www.ifs.org.uk/publications/9164

IPPR (Institute for Public Policy Research) (2018) *Prosperity and justice: A plan for the new economy – The final report of the IPPR Commission on Economic Justice*, Cambridge: Polity Press.

Jerrim, J. and Vignoles, A. (2015) 'Socioeconomic differences in children's test scores: what we do know, what we don't know and what we need to know', *Longitudinal and Life Course Studies*, 6(3): 331–76.

Joyce, R. and Sibieta, L. (2013) 'An assessment of Labour's record on income inequality and poverty', *Oxford Review of Economic Policy*, 29(1): 178–202.

JRF (Joseph Rowntree Foundation) (2018) *Destitution in the UK*, York: JRF.

Kamerman, S. and Kahn, A.J. (1997) *Family change and family policies in Great Britain, Canada, New Zealand, and the United States*, Oxford: Clarendon Press.

Keillor, G. (1974) *Prairie Home Companion*. Minneapolis: Minnesota Public Radio.

Kelley, N., Warhurst, C. and Wishart, R. (2018) 'Work and welfare, "The changing face of the UK labour market"', in D. Phillips, J. Curtice, M. Phillips and J. Perry (eds) *British social attitudes: The 35th report*, London: NatCen Social Research.

Kelly, E., Lee, T., Sibieta, L. and Waters, T. (2018) *Public spending on children in England: 2000 to 2020*, Institute for Fiscal Studies, London: Children's Commissioner for England.

Kelly, G. (2018) *We can't all be winners as a new welfare state emerges*, Observer newspaper, 28 October.

Kiernan, K.E. and Mensah, F.K. (2011) 'Poverty, family resources and children's early educational attainment: the mediating role of parenting', *British Educational Research Journal*, 37(2): 317–36.

Labour Party (1997) *New Labour because Britain deserves better*, Cheam: HH Associates.

Labour Party (2001) *Ambitions for Britain: Labour's manifesto for 2001*, Sutton: HH Associates.

Law, J., Charlton, J. and Asmussen, K. (2017) *Language as a child wellbeing indicator*, London: Early Intervention Foundation.

Leadsom, A., Field, F., Burstow, P. and Lucas, C. (2014) *The 1001 critical days*, London: Department for Education.

Lewis, C. and Lamb, M.E. (2009) *Fathers and fatherhood: Connecting the strands of diversity*, York: Policy Research Bureau and Joseph Rowntree Foundation.

Lewis, J. (2007) 'Teenagers and their parents: parental time and parenting style – what are the issues?', *Political Quarterly*, 78(2): 292–300.

Lindsey, G., Cullen, M.A., Cullen, S., Totsika, V., Bakopoulou, I., Goodlad, S., Brind, R., Pickering, E., Bryson, C., Purdon, S., Conlon, G. and Mantovani, I. (2014) 'CANparent trial evaluation: final report research report', CEDAR, University of Warwick.

Maplethorpe, N., Chalfreau, J., Philo, D. and Tait, C. (2010) *Families with children in Britain: Findings from the 2008 Families and Children Study (FACS)*, London: Department of Work and Pensions.

Marmot, M. (2010) *Fair society, healthy lives, the Marmot review, strategic review of health inequalities in England post-2010*, London: The Marmot Review.

Marmot, M., Stansfeld, S., Patel, C., North, F., Head, J., White, I., Brunner, E., Feeney, A. and Davey Smith, G. (1991) 'Health inequalities among British civil servants: the Whitehall II study', *The Lancet*, 337(8754): 1387–93.

Masarik, A.S. and Conger, R.D. (2017) 'Stress and child development: a review of the family stress model', *Current Opinion in Psychology*, 13: 85–90.

May, T. (2016) First speech as Prime Minister, 13 July.

Ministry of Housing, Communities and Local Government (2019) *Evaluation of the Troubled Families Programme 2015–2020: Findings overview policy report*, London: OCG Crown copyright.

Ministry of Justice (2011) *The Family justice review final report,* London; Crown copyright.

Munro, E. (2011) *The Munro review of child protection: A child centred system: Final report*, Norwich: TSO.

National Audit office (2018) *Rolling out Universal Credit*, London: House of Commons.

National Equality Panel (2010) *An anatomy of economic inequality in the UK*, London: Government Equalities Office.

National Evaluation of Sure Start Team (2010) *The impact of Sure Start local programmes on child development and family functioning: Report of the longitudinal study of 5-year-old children and their families*, London: DfE.

National Scientific Council on the Developing Child (2007) *The science of early childhood development: Closing the gap between what we know and what we do,* Available at: www.developingchild.harvard.edu

Nieuwenhuis, R. and Maldonado, L. (2018) *The triple bind of single parent families: Resources, employment and policies to improve wellbeing,* Bristol: Policy Press.

Oates, J., Karmiloff-Smith, A. and Johnson, M. (2012) *Developing brains,* Early Childhood in Focus, Milton Keynes: Open University.

O'Connor, T.G. and Scott S.B.C. (2007) *Parenting and outcomes for children,* York: Joseph Rowntree Foundation.

ONS (Office for National Statistics) (2013) 'Census 2011', Table 1301EW.

ONS (2017) 'Statistical bulletin, families and households'.

ONS (2019) 'UK Economics Accounts time series' (UKEA).

Park, A. and Rhead, R. (2013) 'Personal relationships, changing attitudes towards sex, marriage and parenthood', in A. Park, C. Bryson, E. Clery, J. Curtice and M. Phillips (eds) *British social attitudes: The 30th report,* London: NatCen Social Research.

Phillips, D., Curtice, J., Phillips, M. and Perry, J. (eds) (2018) *British social attitudes: The 35th report,* London: NatCen Social Research.

Phoenix, A. and Husain, F. (2007) *Parenting and ethnicity,* London: Joseph Rowntree Foundation.

Putnam, R.D. (2015) *Our kids, the American dream in crisis,* New York, NY: Simon and Shuster.

Resolution Foundation (2018) *How to spend it: Autumn Budget 2018 response,* London: Resolution Foundation.

Respect Task Force (2006) *Respect action plan,* London: Home Office.

Richards, L., Garratt, E. and Heath, A.F., with Anderson, L. and Altintaş, E. (2016) *The childhood origins of social mobility: Socio-economic inequalities and changing opportunities,* London: Social Mobility Commission.

Romeo, R., Leonard, J., Robinson, S., West, M., Mackey, A., Row, M. and Gabrieli, J. (2018) 'Beyond the 30-million-word gap: children's conversational exposure is associated with language-related brain function', *Association for Psychological Science,* 1–11.

Ruhm, C. and Waldfogel, J. (2011) 'Long-term effects of early childhood care and education', IZA DP No. 6149.

Rutter, M., Giller, H. and Hagel, A. (1998) *Antisocial behaviour by young people*, Cambridge: Cambridge University Press.

Sammons, P., Sylva, K., Melhuish, E., Siraj, I., Taggart, B., Toth, K. and Smees, R. (2014) *Influences on students' GCSE attainment and progress at age 16. Effective Pre-School, Primary & Secondary Education Project (EPPSE) research report*, London: Department for Education.

Sammons, P., Halls, J., Smees, R. and Goff, J. (2015) 'The impact of children's centres: studying the effect of children's centres in promoting better outcomes for children and their families. Evaluation of Children's Centres in England (ECCE Strand 4)', research brief.

Schmid, K., Al Ramiah, A. and Hewstone, M. (2014) 'Neighborhood ethnic diversity and trust, the role of intergroup contact and perceived threat', *Psychological Science*, 25(3) p 670.

Schoon, I., Cheng, H., Jones, E. and Maughan, B. (2013) *Wellbeing of children: Early influences*, London: Institute of Education and Social Research, King's College, London Institute of Psychiatry and Nuffield Foundation.

Schoon, I., (2018), *Supporting Youth Transitions: The role of parenting and family structures understood within a wider context,* Paper presented at an Expert Group meeting organised by The Doha International Family Institute (DIFI) in collaboration with the United Nations Division for Inclusive Social Development of the Department of Economic and Social affairs (UNDESA) and the International Federation for Family Development (IFFD). 11-12 December 2018 in Doha, Qatar.

Sefton, T. (2004) *A fair share of welfare, public spending on children in England*, Case Report 25, London: London School of Economics.

Seldon, A. and Snowdon, P. (2016) *Cameron at 10, the verdict*, London: William Collins.

SETF (Social Exclusion Task Force) (2007) *Reaching out think family: Analysis and themes from the Families at Risk Review*, London: Cabinet Office.

SETF (2008) *Think family: Improving the life chances of families at risk*, London: Cabinet Office.

Shaw, B., Menzies, L., Bernardes, E. and Baars, S. (2016) *Ethnicity, gender and social mobility*, London: Department for Education.

Shelter (2013) *Growing up renting: A childhood spent in private rented homes*, London: Shelter.

Shonkoff, J.P. and Phillips, D.A. (eds) (2000) *From neurons to neighborhoods: The science of early childhood development*, Washington, DC: National Academy Press.

Siraj-Blatchford, I. and Siraj-Blatchford, J. (2009) *Improving developmental outcomes for children through effective practice in integrating early years services*, London: Centre for Excellence in Outcomes in Children's and Young People's Services.

Smith, G., Sylva, K., Smith, T. and Sammons, P. (2018) *STOP START, survival, decline or closure? Children's centres in England, 2018*, London: Sutton Trust.

Social Justice Policy Group (2006) *Breakdown Britain*, London: Centre for Social Justice.

Social Metrics Commission (2018) *A new measure of poverty for the UK*, final report of the Social Metrics Commission chaired by Baroness Philippa Stroud, London: Social Metrics Commission.

Social Mobility Commission (2017) *Time for change: An assessment of government policies on social mobility 1997–2017*, London: Social Mobility Commission.

Social Mobility Commission (2019) *State of the nation 2018–19, social mobility in Great Britain*, London: Social Mobility Commission.

Stewart, K. (2013) *Social policy in a cold climate, Working Paper No 4, Labour's record on the under fives: Policy, spending and outcomes 1997–2010*, July, London: Joseph Rowntree Foundation, Nuffield Foundation and Trust for London, p 5.

Stewart, K. and Obolenskaya, P. (2016) 'Young children', in Lupton, R., Burchardt, T., Stewart, K., Vizard, P., (eds) *Social policy in a cold climate: Policies and their consequences since the crisis*, Bristol: Policy Press.

Stewart, K., Cooper, K. and Shutes, I. (2019) *What does Brexit mean for social policy in the UK? An exploration of the potential consequences of the 2016 referendum for public services, inequalities and social rights*, SPDO Research Paper 3, London: CASE, London School of Economics.

Sylva, K., Melhuish, T., Sammons, P., Siraj-Blatchford, I. and Tagartt, B. (eds) (2010) *Early childhood matters, evidence from the Effective Pre-School and Primary Education Project*, Abingdon: Routledge.

Sylva, K., Sammons, P., Siraj, I., Taggart, B., Mathers, S. and Melhuish, T. (2017) 'Do graduates and ratings really make no difference?', *Nursery World*, 6 March.

Taylor, M. (2017) 'Good work: the Taylor review of modern working practices', Department for Business, Energy and Industrial Strategy.

Timmins, N. (1996) *The five giants, a biography of the welfare state*, London: Fontana Press, an imprint of HarperCollins Publishers.

Vizard, P., Burchardt, T., Obolenskaya, P., Shutes, I. and Battaglini, B. (2018) *Child poverty and multidimensional disadvantage: Tackling 'data exclusion' and extending the evidence base on 'missing' and 'invisible' children overview report*, CASE Report 114, London: LSE, Centre for the Analysis of Social Exclusion.

Waldfogel, J. (2006) *What children need*, Boston, MA: Harvard University Press.

Washbrook, E. and Waldfogel, J. (2008) 'Early years policy', paper presented at Carnegie Corporation of New York and Sutton Trust conference on social mobility and education, New York.

Washbrook, E., Gregg, P. and Propper, C. (2014) 'A decomposition analysis of the relationship between parental income and multiple child outcomes', *Journal of the Royal Statistical Society*, 177(4): 757–82.

Waters, T. (2018) *Personal tax and benefit measures*, presentation at IFS Budget briefing, London: Institute for Fiscal Studies.

Waylen, A. and Stewart-Brown, S. (2008) *Diversity, complexity and change in parenting*, York: Joseph Rowntree Foundation.

Wellings, K., Palmer, M., Geary, R. et al (2016) 'Changes in conceptions in women younger than 18 years and the circumstances of young mothers in England in 2000–12: an observational study', *Lancet*. Available at: http://dx.doi.org/10.1016/S0140-6736(16)30449-4

Wickham, S., Whitehead, M., Taylor-Robinson, D. and Barr, B. (2017) 'The effect of a transition into poverty on child and maternal mental health: a longitudinal analysis of the UK Millennium Cohort Study', *The Lancet Public Health*, 2(3): e141–e148.

Wilkinson, R. and Marmot, M. (eds) (2003) *Social determinants of health: The solid facts* (2nd edn), Copenhagen: World Health Organisation.

Wilkinson, R. and Pickett, K. (2009) *The spirit level: why equality is better for everyone*, London: Allen Lane.

Willetts, D. (2010) *The pinch – How baby-boomers took their children's future, and why they should give it back*, London: Atlantic Books.

Zaranko, B. (2018) *An end to austerity?*, presentation at IFS Budget briefing, London: Institute for Fiscal Studies.

Index

Page numbers followed by *f* refer to figures and by *t* refer to tables.

'Welfare Society' 86
welfare state 14
What Works Centres 89, 90, 108, 147
Willett, D., *The pinch – How baby-boomers took their children's future, and why they should give it back* 153
worklessness
  benefit spending 128
  and child poverty 20–1
  ethnic groups 24
  indicators of impact 100–1
  language skills and 36
  New Deal and 71
  recession and 83

reduction in 20, 95, 138
and relationship distress 52, 122
as risk 58, 59–60, 61–3
social attitudes to 28–9

Y

Youth Endowment Fund 101
youth justice 73
youth violence 101

Z

zero-hours contracts 21